AR
OF THE WEST

Other titles in the Stackpole Military History Series

ARMY
OF THE WEST

The Weekly Reports of German Army Group B from Normandy to the West Wall

Edited by James A. Wood

STACKPOLE
BOOKS

Published by
STACKPOLE BOOKS
5067 Ritter Road
Mechanicsburg, PA 17055
www.stackpolebooks.com

Maps by Lyle Wood

Cover design by Tracy Patterson

Printed in the United States of America

10 9 8 7 6 5 4 3 2 1

Library of Congress Cataloging-in-Publication Data

Army of the West : the weekly reports of German Army Group B from
Normandy to the west wall / edited by James A. Wood. — 1st ed.
    p. cm. — (Stackpole Military History Series)
  Includes bibliographical references and index.
  ISBN-13: 978-0-8117-3404-2
  ISBN-10: 0-8117-3404-8
  1. Germany. Heeresgruppe B—History. 2. World War, 1939–1945—
Regimental histories—Germany. 3. World War, 1939–1945—Campaigns—
Western Front. I. Wood, James A., 1978–

D757.1.A74 2007
940.54'1343—dc22
                                        2007019666

Table of Contents

Introduction

In May 1944, the headquarters of the German Seventh and Fifteenth Armies and the command staff of the Northern Military District in Holland received messages from Lieutenant General Hans Speidel at Army Group B headquarters in La Roche–Guyon. As Field Marshal Rommel's chief of staff, Speidel was writing to request a weekly situation report from his subordinate army commands, to be received at headquarters by noon on Sunday of each week. These accounts would then be compiled into a single combined report for the Army Group and submitted to the German Armed Forces High Command (*Oberkommando der Wehrmacht*, or OKW).

These weekly situation reports provided to Army Group B headquarters were to follow a set format (see below) and provide a general estimate of the situation, followed by detailed reports on a variety of subjects. These details were to include the progress of defensive construction in the coastal areas, where work on the Atlantic Wall was moving ahead at an accelerated pace in preparation for the impending Allied invasion. Army commanders were also requested to report enemy air and sea operations in the region, noting any damage or casualties inflicted by Allied aircraft in bombing or strafing raids. Finally, reports were to provide an assessment of civilian attitudes in the occupied territories, noting any incidents of sabotage or resistance that might have occurred.

Reports completed prior to the Allied invasion of June 6 emphasize the progress of defensive construction along the coast and in the interior. Following the landings in Normandy, the reports provide a glimpse of the fighting from the German perspective and capture the frustrations of German commanders as they struggled to stem the Allied advance. As their requests for reinforcements were consistently ignored or denied by higher headquarters, reports from the Normandy front increasingly betray a growing sense of hopelessness on the part of German commanders. Citing Allied air superiority and the seemingly unlimited amounts of ammunition available to the enemy, they elaborated on the difficulty of the situation and urged a withdrawal to more defensible positions east of the Seine.

As the campaign wore on, the standard format of the early reports broke down as a succession of German commanders was appointed to the command of Army Group B. Prior to the invasion, Rommel's reports were often accompanied by requests for greater authority, part of an effort by the "Desert Fox" to secure command of the panzer divisions that he considered necessary if Germany were to prevent the Allies from securing a foothold on the continent. These requests for reinforcements and greater authority continued after the Allied landings, although it became increasingly clear that Rommel doubted the possibility of driving the enemy from the bridgehead. In July, Rommel suffered severe injuries when his car was driven off the road by attacking Allied aircraft. He was subsequently succeeded in command of Army Group B by Field Marshal Günther von Kluge.

Von Kluge arrived in Normandy confident of his ability to turn the tide of the battle and restore the situation, but before long he too became convinced that the campaign in the west was lost. Falling under suspicion after the failure of the July 20 attempt to assassinate Hitler, von Kluge felt compelled to present his reports as a statement of his own commitment to the cause, tempered by an unspoken admission that all hope for victory was gone. Recalled to Berlin in August, von Kluge instead chose suicide and was replaced by Field Marshal Walter Model.

As "Hitler's fireman," the man who halted the Red Army's advance before the gates of Warsaw, Model, like von Kluge before him, arrived from the Eastern Front determined to set things right in the west and stop the Allies in their tracks. Appointed to the command of Army Group B at Hitler's personal request, Model enjoyed direct access to the Führer, and this is reflected in his letters. Dropping all pretense of an orderly situation report, Model's reports from the front were informal, direct, and often submitted with the request that they be delivered directly to the Führer.

The reports included in this collection are divided chronologically into six chapters. Brief summaries are included in each section to provide the context in which these reports were written. Also included are brief biographical entries for several of the key German commanders whose names are referred to in these reports, from Keitel at OKW down to the various divisional commanders in the Seventh, Fifteenth, and Fifth Panzer Armies. The original translation of these weekly situation reports was completed shortly after the surrender of Germany by Allied authorities working from captured documents. Sections missing from this translation have been recovered from microfilmed copies of the German originals. Although these reports have been arranged into tables for ease of use, the information provided in the tables remains unchanged. In the tables that provide current figures alongside those of the previous week, figures for the week before have been placed in brackets.

FORMAT FOR WEEKLY SITUATION REPORTS BY GERMAN ARMY COMMANDERS IN NORMANDY
SECRET

Teletype to:
Northern Military District
15th Army Headquarters
7th Army Headquarters

A weekly report is to be made by noon each Sunday to Army Group in the following form:

I Estimate of the situation in general
II Report on and estimate of the enemy situation.
   (a) Ground
   (b) Sea
   (c) Air
   (d) Internal situation

III In detail
  A Coastal defences (alterations)
    (a) Organization of defence
    (b) Construction of Atlantic Wall
      (1) Fortifications completed
      (2) Approximate percentage of the whole project completed
      (3) Progress of construction and particular defects
      (4) Labour employed:
        (a) Soldiers
        (b) Civilians
    (c) Consolidation of the land front
  B Enemy operations on the coast
  C Operations of enemy aircraft
    (1) (a) Bombing raids
      (b) Strafing raids
      (c) Focal point of attacks
      (d) Total of attacks directed against:
        (aa) Positions
        (bb) Building sites
        (cc) Transport targets
        (dd) Airfields
    (2) Casualties:
      (a) Soldiers killed
      (b) Soldiers wounded
      (c) German civilians killed
      (d) German civilians wounded
      (e) French civilians killed
      (f) French civilians injured
    (3) Losses in material
      (a) In attacks on positions
      (b) In attacks on buildings under construction
      (c) In attacks on transport targets
      (d) Unserviceable airfields (in brackets, airfields attacked in the preceding week, and not yet made serviceable)
      (e) In attacks on airfields
      (f) In other attacks

(4) Aircraft losses:
  (a) Enemy
  (b) Own
D (1) Feeling and behaviour of the civilian population
  (2) Instances of sabotage
    (a) Against railways
    (b) Against cables
    (c) Against crops
    (d) Against soldiers
    (e) Attacks with use of explosives
    (f) Cases of arson
    (g) Others

> Army Group B High Command,
> The Chief of General Staff,
>
> Speidel,
> Lieutenant-General.

CHAPTER 1

Preparations for the Invasion and the Atlantic Wall, May 15–June 5, 1944

In 1942, Hitler dreamed of a 3,000-mile fortified coast, a European fortress that would block any attempt by the Western Allies to gain a foothold on the continent. The Atlantic Wall of his fortress was to consist of a line of static coastal defenses running from Norway to the Spanish-French border. It was upon this barrier that the Führer and his military advisors intended to base the German defense of occupied Europe. Construction of the wall began in 1942, with Hitler himself taking an active interest in all aspects of the undertaking, down to the most minute details of pillbox design and concrete casement construction. Concentrating the strongest of these defenses in the areas most threatened by the enemy, and especially the English Channel coast between the Seine and Scheldt Rivers, massive coastal artillery emplacements were positioned overlooking key ports, such as Calais, Dunkirk, and Boulogne. Even if the British and Americans did not come in 1942, Hitler believed that before the war was over, Germany would have to face down an Allied invasion of northwest Europe. The outcome of this battle would be decisive: once the landings were defeated and the invasion repelled, victory in the west would allow the redeployment of German forces to the Eastern Front and perhaps bring an end to the war on terms favorable to Germany.

As the war dragged on and German forces suffered cata-strophic defeats in other theaters, Hitler became increasingly convinced that the decisive battle of the war would be fought in the west. By November 1943 he had become so concerned by the threat of an Anglo-American invasion that he issued Führer Directive 51, ordering the reinforcement of German defenses in the west.[1]

It was at this time that Hitler recalled Field Marshal Erwin Rommel from Italy and appointed him to conduct an inspec-tion of European coastal defenses. During these inspections, Rommel was to report directly to the Führer on the strength of the Atlantic Wall, and upon the completion of this tour, Rom-mel was placed in command of Army Group B, which included the German Seventh and Fifteenth Armies. As Commander-in-Chief (C-in-C) of Army Group B, responsible for strengthen-ing coastal defenses in northwest Europe, Rommel's new command was limited to the coastal belt stretching six miles inland from the shoreline. Any measures that involved opera-tional movement, and especially the movement of mobile and armored divisions, therefore required the approval of C-in-C West, Field Marshal Gerd von Rundstedt.

Following his assignment to the Western Theater, Rommel made a series of visits to construction sites where military and civilian personnel were busily installing beach defenses, pour-ing concrete, and erecting glider obstacles known as "Rommel's asparagus." Under his command, units engaged in construction work consumed all of the concrete and steel that could be pro-vided to them, completing thousands of bunkers and other fortifications. Rommel also ordered a staggering increase in mine-laying activity during this period, and although he received only five million of the 50–100 million mines

---

[1] Gordon A. Harrison, *Cross-Channel Attack*, United States Army in World War II Series: The European Theater of Operations (Washington, DC: Center of Military History, United States Army, 1989), 464–67; F. H. Hins-ley, et al., *British Intelligence in the Second World War: Its Influence on Strategy and Operations*, vol. 3, pt. 2 (London: Her Majesty's Stationery Office, 1988), 33.

requested, the rate of mine-laying under Rommel's command increased to almost triple that of the previous three years.[2]

While this construction was in progress, a dispute developed between Field Marshals von Rundstedt and Rommel. At the root of this disagreement—an argument which was to have a significant impact on the German response to the Allied invasion—was the issue of how best to distribute the panzer divisions that would serve as a mobile reserve behind the line of coastal fortifications.[3] Von Rundstedt adhered to the traditional view that an effective defense would require German armored forces to be kept well back from the coast and held in readiness for a counterattack once the focal point of the enemy invasion had been determined. Remembering the *blitzkrieg* successes of 1939–40, von Rundstedt intended to smash through the enemy in the open country beyond the beaches and then push the invaders back into the sea. Von Rundstedt's ideas were firmly supported by Field Marshal Geyr von Schweppenburg, the commander of Panzer Group West. Rommel, taking the opposite view, argued that von Rundstedt's ideas were the result of his lack of experience in fighting under Allied air superiority. Drawing from his experiences in North Africa, Rommel firmly believed that the devastating power of Allied air attacks would disrupt the movement of German reserve forces to the front lines and thereby prevent distant panzer divisions from mounting a successful counterattack. He was convinced that the invasion had to be stopped on the beaches as Allied airpower would prevent the movement of reinforcements as required by von Rundstedt's plan. Instead, Rommel wanted to form local reserves of individual panzer divisions, stationed close behind the beaches and capable of mounting immediate counterat-

---

[2] Blumenson, "Rommel," in Corelli Barnett, *Hitler's Generals* (New York: Grove Weidenfeld, 1989), 310; C. P. Stacey, *The Victory Campaign. The Operations in North-West Europe, 1944–1945*, vol. 3, Official History of the Canadian Army in the Second World War (Ottawa: The Queen's Printer and Controller of Stationery, 1960), 56.

[3] Stacey, 55.

tacks in the event of an Allied landing.[4] Von Rundstedt, however, believed that Rommel's dispersion of forces along a thin defensive line would be too easily pierced and would prevent the widely-dispersed armored formations from massing their strength against the Allied landings. Dispersed along the coast, these armored divisions would only be demolished by Allied naval guns and airpower.[5]

In the months that followed, both commanders remained adamant and were unable to reach an agreement. Frustrated and unable secure approval for his plans by acting within the chain of command, Rommel carried his appeal directly to Hitler. In response, the Führer imposed a solution that satisfied no one: he agreed with Rommel's plan to distribute panzer divisions along the coastline, but he also saw the merits of von Rundstedt's argument for the need for a substantial armored reserve. As a compromise solution, on April 26, 1944, Hitler divided the reserve forces between von Rundstedt and Rommel with three divisions each.[6] The Führer also established a mobile reserve of four divisions under his personal control, which would be kept well back from the coast under the command of Geyr von Schweppenburg. With the 21st Panzer Division remaining on the Normandy front, the remainder would be held at intervals along the coast or stationed in southern France.

Neither of the two commanders was satisfied by this decision. There were too few mobile reserves to have the shock effect that von Rundstedt wanted and too few stationed near the coast to fulfill Rommel's plan to stop the invaders on the beaches. All motorized vehicles in the theater were put under the command of Geyr von Schweppenburg's Panzer Group West, but these required Hitler's approval for release. Rommel was therefore denied direct control of the panzer divisions of OKW reserve, a control he felt necessary for a quick counterattack that would stop the invasion on the beaches. He had at his

[4] OKW, "War Diary (1 Apr–18 Dec 1944)," MS# B-034 in *World War II: German Military Studies*, vol. 10, pt. 4 (New York: Garland Publishing, 1979), 6.

[5] Ziemke, "Rundstedt," in Barnett, ed., 199.

[6] OKW, 10.

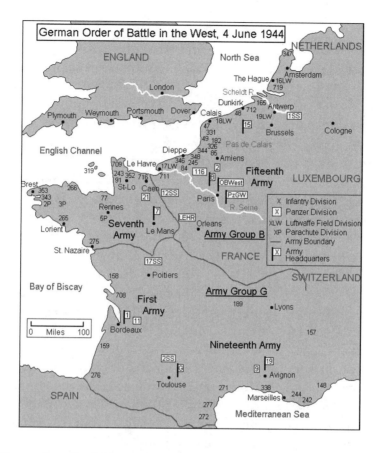

German Order of Battle in the West, 4 June 1944

disposal only three armored divisions (the 21st, 2nd, and 116th Panzer Divisions) to cover the entire coastline from the Loire to the Scheldt. As events would show, only 21st Panzer stood within immediate reach of the Normandy invasion beaches. Von Rundstedt's sixty divisions—thirty-five of which were under Rommel's command and only ten of which were armored—had three thousand miles of coastline to defend. The half-measure adopted by Hitler, arguably the result of his obsession with maintaining divided authority within the Third Reich, would ultimately impede the German Army's response to the Allied invasion of 1944.[7]

---

[7] Carlo D'Este, *Decision in Normandy* (New York: Konecky & Konecky, 1994), 506; Stacey, 61, 70; Max Hastings, *Overlord: D-Day and the Battle for Normandy* (New York: Simon & Schuster, 1984), 64.

The day of invasion was fast approaching. On May 15, Generals Dwight D. Eisenhower and Bernard Montgomery were presenting the final plans for Operation OVERLORD to a gathering of Allied commanders at St. Paul's Cathedral in London. During this presentation, Monty was full of confidence and showed absolute mastery of the plan to invade at Normandy.[8]

Although the Germans knew the invasion would come, they did not know when or where. Signals intelligence was not helping, providing little besides a series of coded messages regarding the First United States Army Group (FUSAG), a fictitious formation that was supposedly posted in East Anglia. These messages were part of Operation FORTITUDE, the ongoing effort to deceive the Germans and draw their attention away from Normandy. Allied radio signals carried out the day-to-day transmissions of what appeared to be an operational army. The assignment of U.S. General George Patton to lead FUSAG provided plenty of publicity to draw attention to its presence. The Germans were convinced that a leader with such a powerful reputation would lead the main force.[9] All German agents in Britain had previously been located by the "Double Cross Committee," rounded up, and given the choice of execution or turning double agent. A steady stream of misinformation now was being sent by radio transmissions to Germany by agents who confirmed the credentials and preparations of FUSAG. German reconnaissance flights over southeast England gave further weight to what was being intercepted on the radio. Here, the Luftwaffe spotted what were actually dummy camps, aircraft, supply depots, tanks, rail lines, landing craft, and even a fake headquarters at Dover, all of which had been constructed of rubber and wood in the months leading up to the landings. By May, German intelligence had identified seventy-nine Allied divisions in Britain, but in fact the Allies had only thirty-seven real divisions, the remainder being Patton's "First Army Group."[10] Most of Fifteenth Army correspondingly

---

[8] D'Este, 90; Hastings, 56.
[9] John Keegan, *Six Armies in Normandy* (New York: Viking-Penguin, 1982), 235.
[10] Stacey, 60; Hinsley, 61.

remained in the Pas de Calais until the first week of August to meet this expected landing that never materialized. Further, FORTITUDE NORTH convinced Hitler that another landing would come in Norway, with the result that twelve German divisions were kept there.[11]

The pattern of Allied bombing in mid-May probably reinforced Hitler's belief that the imminent invasion would come in the Pas de Calais rather than Normandy. To keep up appearances, for every bomb dropped on rail lines, transportation centers, and military industrial installations in Normandy, there were two bombs dropped near Calais. Bombing became especially intensive after May 21, when British and American aircraft launched Operation CHATTANOOGA CHOO-CHOO, a systematic attack on rail lines, railway engines, rolling stock, marshalling and repair yards, bridges, and tunnels throughout northern France.[12] Between May 7 and May 28, seventy-four bridges and tunnels were destroyed. Synthetic oil plants in Germany became the next targets, with the hope that the German Army would not be able to produce the fuel necessary to operate their aircraft, tanks and industries.

The Allies were able to track the success of their deception scheme through ULTRA decrypts.[13] The Germans were not aware that the Allies had captured one of their Enigma transmission machines and had broken their codes. At this time, nearly six thousand encrypters were engaged in a top-secret program at Bletchley Park near London to intercept transmissions from German command posts and headquarters, as well as to send out FORTITUDE transmissions from the Double Cross agents. In May, ULTRA decoded Rommel's warning to German High Command that the systematic Allied destruction of railways throughout Northern France had begun to disrupt his supply and troop movements. ULTRA also allowed the Allies to confirm that the Germans still did not know where the landings would fall.[14]

---

[11] Richard Overy, *Why the Allies Won* (New York: W. W. Norton & Company, 1995), 151.

[12] Harrison, 230.

[13] D'Este, 122, 167, 237, 416.

[14] Hinsley, 60–61, 64, 75, 79–80.

The Allies used these decrypts to pinpoint the existence, location, and movement of German troops and military formations. They intercepted messages showing that the Luftwaffe had lost more than three thousand pilots since the beginning of the year, either killed in action or taken prisoner. They also learned that Rommel had been refused permission to station reserve forces able to cover Brittany and Normandy simultaneously—thus learning that the areas behind the American landing beaches would not be guarded at full strength.[15] On May 25, British intelligence passed on two significant messages: first, Rommel's complaint of May 19 that one SS panzer division had no tanks, was not expecting any, and was short of officers, motor transport, and spare vehicles. Also decrypted was a German Air Force message expecting the landings to go ashore near Dieppe. On May 26, Rommel's message of two weeks earlier was decrypted, warning that the locomotive situation was so serious that forced labor and even prisoners of war would have to be used at the repair shops. Later in May, ULTRA messages also revealed a considerable transfer of troops to the Cotentin peninsula,[16] forcing the Americans to revise their plan for a paratroop drop at La Haye-du-Puits.

As D-Day approached, Allied bombardment became even more intense.[17] In March and April, eight thousand British bombers dropped forty-two thousand tons of bombs. This was later stepped up to eleven thousand tons dropped by U.S. bombers in May. Railway marshalling yards and fortifications along the Atlantic Wall were the main targets, but on May 28, the destruction of Chateau Terlinden, a German wireless station near Bruges, made it much more difficult for German intelligence to detect the extra volume of wireless traffic that would immediately precede the landings.[18] A second wireless intercept station was also destroyed on the night of the inva-

---

[15] Harrison, 257.

[16] Hinsley, 81, 86.

[17] Hinsley, 115–17.

[18] Martin Gilbert, *Second World War*, new ed. (London: Phoenix Press, 2000), 529.

sion, wiping out communications in the vital Cherbourg area. An air raid over northern France cut the Luftwaffe overland telephone cable between Paris and Rouen, interrupting telephone communications between the headquarters in Paris and air forces around Caen and Rennes for three crucial days leading up to the landings.

Bad weather in the first week of June forced Eisenhower in the early hours of June 4 to postpone the landings set for June 5 to the following day.[19] Von Rundstedt, meanwhile, sent a radio signal to Berlin stating that the Allies would need four consecutive days of decent weather in order to carry out a cross-channel assault. With no such four-day period in the immediate forecast, he believed that no invasion could take place in the first week of June. His message was decrypted at Bletchley Park and immediately passed on to Eisenhower. The weather worsened on June 3, with German forecasters predicting three to four days of continued bad weather. Allied forecasting, however, was more precise, owing to the capture of German weather stations in Iceland, Greenland, Spitzbergen, and Jan Mayen Island. On June 4, the Allies were forecasting a brief spell of clearing weather, while at the same time, German naval command in Paris was reporting that an invasion could not be considered imminent. At 9:45 P.M., Eisenhower at Supreme Headquarters Allied Expeditionary Force (SHAEF) made the decision to go.[20] Rommel, however, was starting his long drive home to Herrlingen, intending to celebrate his wife Lucie's birthday on June 6 before continuing on for a meeting with Hitler where he would request two additional panzer divisions, an anti-aircraft corps, and further reinforcements.

✠

---

[19] Hinsley, 125.
[20] D'Este, 110; Harrison, 274.

WEEKLY REPORT, MAY 15–20, 1944

I Estimate of the situation as a whole

After a decrease in enemy air activity from May 15 until the morning of May 19, probably imposed by weather conditions, heavy enemy air attacks against coastal defenses and rear areas (transport targets, Luftwaffe installations) were resumed from midday, May 19, and continued without respite on May 20.

Enemy air reconnaissance was concentrated on the Channel coast, in particular on both sides of the Canche and Somme estuaries, over Cotentin and the north-western area of Brittany. No results of our own air reconnaissance of the island during the time covered by the report are available, and consequently only an incomplete estimate of the enemy situation is possible.

Continuation of invasion preparations includes air reconnaissance of beach defenses.

Our own defensive power has been increased by completing regrouping in the Netherlands, in the Cotentin, and in the Brittany area, and by increased fortification and mining.

II Report and estimate of the enemy situation

(a) Ground

Concentrations in southern and south-eastern England again confirmed by the location of Montgomery's H.Q. south of London, and by the transfer of a British division from northern to south-eastern England, and of an American division from Northern Ireland to the south of England. The enemy has carried out reconnaissance of beach defenses north-east of Calais and at the estuary of the Somme. According to the statement of prisoners, coastal reconnaissance extending to from Holland to Normandy has been proceeding for almost the last two months, and probably includes reconnaissance of land minefields with new types of mines. The possibility that the enemy is informed at least about earlier types of beach defenses must be taken into account.

(b) Sea

Since about May 7 it has been noted that a large formation of tank-landing craft has been transferred from western England (Liverpool?) along the south coast as far as Harwich. It is not clear whether this is a practice maneuver or part of the strategical plan.

According to a prisoner's statement on May 20, there is supposed to be a large number of landing craft in the area between Eastbourne and Brighton. There has been a great deal of mining in the Hook of Holland area. Repeated explosions have been noted to the west of the Dutch Coast, which are probably the results of enemy minesweeping operations.

Strict enemy surveillance of the central Channel by destroyers and motor gunboats is presumably directed against German motor torpedo boats.

(c) Air

Following an improvement in the weather, the enemy Air Force attacked coastal defenses with strong formations on the afternoon of May 19 and 20, and also transport targets and Luftwaffe installations (airfields and radar installations), particularly in the area of northern France behind the line Calais-Dieppe, and in the area of Greater Paris. Considerable damage was caused to three transport installations and to airfields. Attacks continue to have little effect against coastal defenses, and these raids cannot be considered yet as a systematic preparation for a large-scale attack.

(d) Internal situation

Increasingly hostile feeling against the enemy powers amongst the population hit by air raids in northern France. Guerilla activities in Brittany have decreased, and combing-out operations continue.

III In detail

Northern Military District:

A. Coastal defenses (Alterations):

(a) Organization of Defense: Coastal Defense Force. 16th Luftwaffe Field Division reinforced on the land front by SS units.

(b) Construction of Atlantic Wall:

Fortifications completed	350 strong points of the winter defense program have been completed, of which 297 are ready for action.
Approximate percentage of the whole project completed	100% completed, 85% ready for action.
Progress of construction and particular defects	Summer schedule advanced, nothing completed. Coastal defenses carried out along 103km., and under construction along 55 km. 50% of air landing stakes planned have been erected. Number of air landing stakes planned increased from 521,000 to 900,000. Lack of building materials of all types.
Labor employed	(a) Soldiers: 1,020 (b) Civilians: 68,090

(c) Consolidation of the land front: 15% of defenses completed, defense of towns carried out with the exception of parts of the anti-tank defenses. Earthworks and defenses commenced on land front.

Shown here at a celebration in Berlin, Adolf Hitler was later to be immersed in preparations for the inevitable Allied invasion of Western Europe. On November 3, 1943, he issued Hitler Directive 51, which ordered the strengthening of German coastal defenses and strongpoints along the 3,000-mile Atlantic Wall. Hitler himself designed the pillboxes and concrete casements for many of the fortifications.

B. Enemy operations on the coast:
    None.

C. Operations of enemy aircraft:

(1)

Bombing raids	None (15)
Strafing raids	4 (7)
Focal point of attacks	Cannot be identified.

Total of attacks directed against:

Positions	None (1)
Building sites	None (0)
Transport targets	None (1)
Airfields	2 (3)

(2) Casualties:

Soldiers killed	0
Soldiers wounded	1
German civilians killed	0
German civilians wounded	0 (0)
French civilians killed	0
French civilians injured	0

(3) Losses in material:

In attacks on positions	Nil return.
In attacks on buildings under construction	Nil return.
In attacks on transport targets	Nil return.
Unserviceable airfields	Nil return.

(4) Aircraft losses:

Enemy	4
Own	2

D.

(1) Feeling and behavior of the civilian population:
Depressed, mostly tired of war, attitude reserved and
expectant.

(2) Instances of sabotage:

Against railways	1
Against cables	None
Against crops	None
Against soldiers	None
Attacks with use of explosives	1
Cases of arson	2
Others	None

15th Army H.Q.:

A. Coastal defenses (Alterations):

(a) Organization of Defense: Unchanged.

(b) Construction of Atlantic Wall: Construction according to
plan. Focal point: beach defenses completed, erection of
air landing stakes, partial lack of cement, wire, hoop iron,
planks and wooden casing frames at G.H.Q. LXVII A.K.

(c) Consolidation of the land front: Construction completed
and ready for action: machine gun, anti-tank, and mortar
positions, blockhouses, dummy positions, and further
dummy minefields laid. Lack of barbed wire and timber.

B. Enemy operations on the coast:

May 17. Attempted reconnaissance of beach defenses at
Les Petites Hommes (to the east of Calais).

May 18. Enemy patrol (2 officers) in rubber dinghy taken
prisoner at Cayeux. Task: Reconnaissance of beach defenses.

C. Operations of enemy aircraft:

(1)

Bombing raids	48 (265)
Strafing raids	16 (50)
Focal point of attacks	See II (c)

Total of attacks directed against:

Positions	10 (34)
Building sites	9 (41)
Transport targets	19 (123)
Airfields	19 (69)

(2) Casualties:

Soldiers killed	6 (130)
Soldiers wounded	10 (315)
German civilians killed	— (48)
German civilians wounded	— (28)
French civilians killed	4 (813)
French civilians injured	9 (1075)

(3) Losses in material:

In attacks on positions	Destroyed: 1 radar installation. Damaged: 8 huts, 1 (radar) site, 5 guns, 1 Würzburg installation, 1 radar installation.
In attacks on buildings under construction	Medium damage: 1 Slightly damaged: 1
In attacks on transport targets	Destroyed: 25 motor cars, 1 lock, railway tracks. Damaged: 3 freight stations, 16 buildings, 1 bridge, 22 motor cars, 1 locomotive, railway tracks, telephone lines, water mains, and electricity cables.

Field Marshal Gerd von Rundstedt was Commander in Chief of the German Army of the West. With sixty divisions under his command, he was charged with stopping the Allied invasion. A respected strategist, von Rundstedt believed in holding the panzer divisions in reserve so that they could be mobilized immediately once the focus of the Allied invasion was determined. The most likely target was believed to be the Pas de Calais region, where twenty divisions of the Fifteenth Army were posted. U.S. HOLOCAUST MEMORIAL MUSEUM

Unserviceable airfields	Epinoy (Maldegham, St. Trond, Grevillers, Couvron, Athis, Wizernes, Melsbroeck Evere, Le Culot, Florennes, Beaumont).
In attacks on airfields	Destroyed: 1 aircraft, 1 runway, 4 hangars, 1 workshop, 2 M/T vehicles, 6 huts, 1 airfield controllers caravan, telephone and electricity cables. Damaged: 1 aircraft, 4 runways, 7 tarmacs, 1 bay, 4 hangars, 1 huts, 1 fire-fighting outfit, telephone and electricity cables.
In other attacks	Destroyed: 3 houses. Damaged: 106 houses, 2 industrial plants, telephone cables, water mains, and electricity cables.

(4) Aircraft losses:

Enemy	6 (71)
Own	— (3)

D.

(1) Feeling and behavior of the civilian population:
   Unchanged, reserved and expectant.

(2) Instances of sabotage:

Against railways	2
Against cables	1
Against crops	—
Against soldiers	2
Attacks with use of explosives	2
Cases of arson	3
Others	—

7th Army H.Q.:

A. Coastal defenses (Alterations):

(a) Organization of Defense: The preparation for defense in Brittany has been strengthened by the arrival of II Paratroop Corps and the 5th Paratroop Division. It has been decided to transfer the reinforcements to Cotentin.

(b) Consolidation report will be sent in later.

B. Enemy operations on the coast:
   None

C. Operations of enemy aircraft:

(1)

Bombing raids	16 (24)
Strafing raids	10 (14)
Focal point of attacks	Artillery positions, meteorological subsidiary station, and Luftwaffe equipment.

Total of attacks directed against:

Positions	10
Building sites	—
Transport targets	7
Airfields	3

(2) Casualties:

Soldiers killed	8 (7 missing)
Soldiers wounded	11
German civilians killed	—
German civilians wounded	2
French civilians killed	—
French civilians injured	Several French civilians injured in the attack on Le Mans.

(3) Losses in material:

In attacks on positions	1 pillbox slightly damaged, 1 gun slightly damaged, 1 hut, 1 dugout, 1 searchlight, 2 motor cars, 1 water tank (1,000 liters).
In attacks on buildings under construction	—

In attacks on transport targets	7 railway tracks, about 30 wagons, about 5 locomotives.
Unserviceable airfields	—
In attacks on airfields	—
In other attacks	1 Luftwaffe locator installation, 1 radio aerial.

(4) Aircraft losses:

Enemy	7
Own	Not known.

D.

(1) Feeling and behavior of the civilian population: Population expects invasion, mood and behavior quiet as before.

(2) Instances of sabotage:

Against railways	2 (no damage)
Against cables	2
Against crops	—
Against soldiers	7
Attacks with use of explosives	1
Cases of arson	—
Others	—

For the Army Group High Command,

The Chief of General Staff,
Speidel

ARMY GROUP B HIGH COMMAND
WEEKLY REPORT, MAY 21–27, 1944

I Estimate of the situation as a whole:

Enemy air activity has greatly increased, but cannot be considered as the final phase of the invasion preparations. Air attacks have, as before, been carried out against coastal defenses and areas to the rear (transport targets, Luftwaffe installations). There has been a striking increase in attacks on radar and locator installations, and especially on bridges.

Enemy air reconnaissance was carried out in the Calais-Cherbourg area and on the west coast of Brittany with no apparent point of concentration.

Our aircraft reconnoitered the harbor areas of Poole, Weymouth, and Portland. An examination of earlier results is necessary to gain a clear estimate of the enemy situation.

Our defense has been reinforced by increased constructional operations and mining. The steady deterioration of the transport situation however is having a bad effect on the situation.

II Report on and estimate of the enemy situation:

(a) Ground
Troop concentrations have been confirmed again in southern and south-east England with the new deposition of 1 American and 2 British divisions.

Since 0200 hours on May 27 there has been complete radio silence.

(b) Sea
On May 24 photographic reconnaissance showed that there are sufficient landing craft in Poole, Weymouth and Portland to transport $2^{1/3}$ landing divisions. There is only a small number of vessels at Folkestone and Dover.

Shown here carrying out an inspection of Atlantic Wall fortifications and holding his field marshal's baton, Erwin Rommel was appointed by Hitler as commander of Army Group B on January 15, 1944. He disagreed with von Rundstedt's views on deployment of the armored reserves. After facing Allied airpower in Africa, he believed it would be necessary to defeat the Allied invasion within the crucial first twenty-four hours. ROYAL MILITARY COLLEGE

Air attacks have been carried out on harbors between Ostend and Fecamp, and also on coastal batteries and radar installations. Only slight damage was caused.

Of 11 naval radar installations damaged, 10 are serviceable again, and 1 can still be repaired. Slight mining activity.

Minelaying is proceeding according to plan on the Dutch coast, but has been made more difficult between Boulogne and Cherbourg owing to losses of torpedo boats, motor boats and barges. The naval depot at Dieppe has been destroyed.

Our E-boat activity has been decreased owing to the weather and mining. Operations by our U-boats off the northern coast of Brittany were unsuccessful because of prompt spotting by the enemy Air Force.

(c) Air

Enemy air activity increased considerably by day, but night operations were hindered in the middle of the week by bad weather conditions in England. Attacks were concentrated in the area between the Somme and Seine estuaries extending to the Paris area, and are still mostly directed against transport (bridges) and Luftwaffe ground organization. Attacks against coastal defenses continue and those against radar and locator installations have increased.

Transport installations have suffered considerable damage; railway stations at Le Mans, Epinal, Chaumont, Orleans, and Montigniers are completely out of action. About 280 locomotives are unserviceable. Several bridges, among them five over the Seine, have been destroyed.

In attacks on airfields there were considerable losses on the ground in 11 cases; 12 airfields are unserviceable.

Attacks on coastal defenses have not resulted in any serious damage. Dummy positions have been attacked several times.

Reconnaissance has been carried out mainly in the area between Calais and Cherbourg, and on the west coast of Brittany.

The quarters and positions of a Landgraf division in the area south of St. Brieue were reconnoitred and attacked.

(d) Internal situation
Considerable feeling against the Anglo-Americans is noticeable amongst the section of the population affected by air raids.

No changes are apparent in the activities of the Resistance organizations. The situation in Brittany remains uncertain.

III In detail:

Northern Military District:

A. Coastal defenses (Alterations):

(a) Organization of Defense: Unchanged.

(b) Construction of Atlantic Wall:

Fortifications completed	Of total schedule 1,218 ready for use, 49 others reinforced with concrete.
Approximate percentage of the whole project completed	67% ready for use, 3% reinforced with concrete.
Progress of construction and particular defects	May 1–25, 73 gun positions reinforced with concrete; a further 48 in course of construction.
Labor employed	(a) Soldiers: 9,550 (b) Civilians: 66,170

(c) Consolidation of the land front: Consolidation of land front proceeding according to plan. Obstacles 25% completed.

B. Enemy operations on the coast:
None.

C. Operations of enemy aircraft:

(1) Number of raids:

Bombing raids	27 (0)
Strafing raids	28 (4)
Focal point of attacks	Transport installation in the Limburg area.

Total of attacks directed against:

Positions	3 (0)
Building sites	0 (0)
Transport targets	26 (0)
Airfields	11 (2)

(2) Casualties:

Soldiers killed	1 (0)
Soldiers wounded	5 (1)
German civilians killed	0 (0)
German civilians wounded	0 (0)
French civilians killed	13 (0)
French civilians injured	29 (0)

(3) Losses in material:

In attacks on positions	None.
In attacks on buildings under construction	None.
In attacks on transport targets	22 locomotives, 7 goods wagons damaged, 1 tug sunk, 1 tug beached, 1 barge (800 tons) burnt out, 9 barges damaged.
Unserviceable airfields	None.
In attacks on airfields	Slight damage to tarmac and buildings, 1 Ju 88 slightly damaged (5%).

This photo of a soldier standing guard beside a long-range anti-invasion gun of the Atlantic Wall appeared in the German *Signal* magazine with the caption, "At the frontier of Europe." Rommel's series of fortifications was enhanced by bunkers, beach obstacles, "asparagus" at potential landing strips, and five million mines. ASSOCIATED PRESS

In other attacks	1 factory heavily damaged, farms and houses destroyed.

(4) Aircraft losses:

Enemy	40
Own	6

D.

(1) Feeling and behavior of the civilian population: The majority of the population expects invasion—in a depressed state of mind. National Socialist propaganda has no effect; the rest are expectant and guided by self-interest.

(2) Instances of sabotage:

Against railways	0

Against cables	0
Against crops	0
Against soldiers	1 Dutch member of the S.S.
Attacks with use of explosives	2
Cases of arson	2
Others	0

15th Army H.Q.:

A. *Coastal defenses (Alterations):*

(a) Organization of Defense: 711th Infantry Division sector strengthened by bringing up 346th Infantry Battalion.

(b) Construction of Atlantic Wall:

Fortifications completed	3 anti-tank positions, 5 anti-aircraft positions, 10 anti-aircraft pillboxes, 1 emplacement, 2 large mine-fields, 2 small minebelts around towns, 76.4 km belt of mines, other firing, machine gun, anti-tank, infantry firing, mortar, field gun positions, foxholes, dugouts for men and munitions, communication trenches, dummy mine-fields, blockhouses.
Approximate percentage of the whole project completed	70%.
Progress of construction and particular defects	According to plan. Supplies of materials lacking: cement, fuel, wooden frames, building materials, tools. Work stoppages owing to air raid alerts.
Labor employed	(a) Soldiers: 27,059 (b) Civilians: 31,966

B. Enemy operations on the coast:

C. Operations of enemy aircraft:

(1) Bomber formations:
Calais–Armentieres–Abbeville–Berck–Cambrai–Ghent–
Liege–Mons–Le Treport–Le Havre, Creil, Bernay, Laon,
Chartres.

Strafing raids: 208 (16)

Reconnaissance: St. Valery–Dieppe–Le Treport–Etaples–
Dunkirk to Ostende.

Fighter and bomber formations: Ghent–Huy–Dinart–
St. Quentin–Fecamp.

Total of attacks directed against:

Positions	53 (10)
Building sites	15 (9)
Transport targets	220 (19)
Airfields	69 (19)

(2) Casualties:

Soldiers killed	61 (6)
Soldiers wounded	156 (10)
German civilians killed	17 (0)
German civilians wounded	35 (0)
French civilians killed	273 (4)
French civilians injured	641 (9)

(3) Losses in material:

In attacks on positions	Destroyed: 3 positions, 3 guns (2 cm. AA), 5 radar installations, 2 Luftwaffe Signals installations, Luftwaffe Signals equipment, cables, 1 building, 1 rotary converter, 1

Soldiers setting up beach obstacles are shown scrambling for cover as an American P-38 passes over on a reconnaissance mission, May 6, 1944. Detailed information on Normandy beach defenses was obtained from photographs like this one, taken near Cherbourg by the U.S. Ninth Army Air Force. U.S. AIR FORCE

	radio station, 7 M/T vehicles, 1,055 litres of fuel burnt. Damaged: 8 buildings and huts, 7 positions, 14 guns (6 of these coastal artillery), 5 radar installations, 2 control plants, 7 pillboxes, receiver of a large radar site, other damage to a barracks.
In attacks on buildings under construction	No damage worth mentioning.
In attacks on transport targets	Destroyed: 4 freight stations, 1 works building, 8 works installations, 1 transformer station, 1 bridge, 33 locomotives, 280 goods wagons, 2 motor cars, 12 trucks, 1 harbor installation, 1 viaduct, 3 vessels.

	Damaged: 5 freight stations, 19 works, 6 works installations, 2 transformer stations, 14 railway bridges, 1 electrical plant, 117 locomotives, several hundred passenger carriages and goods wagons, 3 motor cars, 6 trucks, 1 harbour installation, 15 vessels and barges, roads, electricity and other cables, tracks.
Unserviceable airfields	(Maldeghem, Wizernes, Epinoy, Arques, Poix-Ost, Cambrai, Ursel, Tirlemont, Diest)
In attacks on airfields	Destroyed: 8 aircraft, 2 aircraft bays, 3 blast bays, 28 hangars, 6 workshops, 8 airfield buildings, 1 M/T vehicle, 38 huts, 1 gun, 11 M/T garages, telephone wires, electricity cables, and water mains. Damaged: 9 aircraft, 2 fuelling installations, 15 runways, 22 tarmacs, 15 aircraft bays, 1 blast bay, 3 hangars, 3 workshops, 16 airfield buildings, 8 boundary lightings, 2 M/T vehicles, 30 huts, 1 gun.
In other attacks	Destroyed: 1 gasometer, several hundred houses (exact figures not possible), 1 crane. Damaged: 6 industrial plants, 5 power stations, 5 gasometers, 1 bridge, 698 houses (in addition, many houses with no details of numbers), electricity and telephone cables.

(4) Aircraft losses:

Enemy	29 (6)
Own	3 (0)

D.

(1) Feeling and behavior of the civilian population: Calm, reserved, expectant, partly upset by air raids.

(2) Instances of sabotage:

Against railways	4
Against cables	8
Against crops	0
Against soldiers	2
Attacks with use of explosives	9
Cases of arson	4
Others	1 attack on German recruiting office.

7th Army H.Q.:

A. Coastal defenses (Alterations):

(a) Organization of Defense: Unchanged.

(b) Construction of Atlantic Wall:

Fortifications completed	15
Approximate percentage of the whole project completed	44,011 cubic meters of reinforced concrete (14.4% of the summer construction program).
Progress of construction and particular defects	Construction is lagging owing to lack of building materials and transport of every description. 159 railway cars of cement were supplied instead

	of 1,600. Partial lack of fuel. The withdrawal of large amounts of workmen is also a handicap.
Labor employed	(a) Soldiers: 2,507 (b) Civilians: 2,336

B. Enemy operations on the coast:

C. Operations of enemy aircraft:

(1) Number of raids:

Bombing raids	53 (16)
Strafing raids	35 (10)
Focal point of attacks	Transport targets, mainly locomotives, supply bases, radar installations.

Total of attacks directed against:

Positions	32 (10)
Building sites	3 (0)
Transport targets	33 (7)
Airfields	6 (3)

(2) Casualties:

Soldiers killed	26 (15)—including 7 missing.
Soldiers wounded	62 (11)
German civilians killed	2
German civilians wounded	7
French civilians killed	4
French civilians injured	0

(3) Losses in material:

In attacks on positions	1 gun destroyed, 1 gun damaged, 1 heavy anti-aircraft

	gun damaged, 1 2 cm. anti-aircraft gun damaged, 1 anti-tank gun damaged.
In attacks on buildings under construction	2 pillboxes damaged, 1 gun damaged.
In attacks on transport targets	53 locomotives, large number of railway cars.
Unserviceable airfields	—
In attacks on airfields	Repair shops and huts.
In other attacks	1 mine-sweeper, 7 radar installations, 2 trucks, 2 field kitchens.

(4) Aircraft losses:

Enemy	21 (in addition, 1 probable) (7)
Own	0

D.

(1) Feeling and behavior of the civilian population: No fresh information.

(2) Instances of sabotage:

Against railways	1 (2)
Against cables	8 (2)
Against crops	0 (0)
Against soldiers	8 (7)
Attacks with use of explosives	1 (1)
Cases of arson	0
Others	0

WEEKLY REPORT, MAY 28–JUNE 3, 1944

I Estimate of the situation as a whole:

The continuation and systematic increase of enemy air attacks and more intensive minelaying in our harbors with improved mining equipment indicate an advance in the enemy's readiness for invasion. Concentration of air attacks on coastal defenses between Dunkirk and Dieppe and on the Seine-Oise bridges confirm the presumed focal point of a large-scale landing, and the possibility that communications may be cut off on the flanks and in the rear. Air reconnaissance of harbors along the entire south coast of England is urgently required. Constructional work on the defense front is being impeded by a further deterioration in the transport situation and of fuel supplies (shortage of coal). The withdrawal of the 19th Luftwaffe Field Division means further weakening of our defense force in the area south of the Scheldt estuary.

II Report on and estimate of the enemy situation:

(a) Ground
Concentrations in southern and south-east England have been confirmed by the location of 2 British armored divisions and 2 American infantry divisions. Radio communication has been normal again in Great Britain since May 30.

Since June 1 the enemy radio has issued an increased number of code words for French Resistance organizations to be at the ready, but from previous experience this cannot be accepted as a hint that the invasion is immediately imminent.

(b) Sea
Air reconnaissance of Dover revealed an unimportant increase in the number of landing craft. The other harbors on the south coast of England were not reconnoitred.

Increased enemy minelaying from the air has been concentrated on the Hook, Calais, Le Havre, St. Nazaire. Some harbours are closed because of enemy mines. Heavy losses have

A reinforced concrete gun emplacement guarding the sea wall near St.-Aubin-sur-Mer, looking eastward and photographed in 1946. Rommel wanted to complete 15,000 fortifications by the time of the invasion. By June 6, 1944, 12,247 bunkers were completed and 500,000 beach obstacles in place. CMHQ HISTORICAL SECTION

been suffered owing to improved enemy mining equipment. Our naval forces are temporarily impeded.

Some enemy targets have been located off our coast, but no actions have been fought with enemy naval forces. Numerous bombing attacks have been made on naval radar installations resulting in some equipment being put out of action, but all location stations are operating again. Naval D/F station Flanders has been destroyed by bombs.

A number of detonations have been heard up to 15 km. off the Dutch coast, presumably enemy minesweeping activity.

(c) Air

Constant enemy air attacks obviously concentrated on bridges over the Seine, Oise, and to a certain extent over the Aisne, also coastal defenses in the Dunkirk-Dieppe sector and on the northern and eastern sides of Cotentin. Attempts to cripple rail transport continue, with raids on marshalling yards (Brussels, Rheims, Ternier, Troyes, Trappes, Saumur and Angers) and on locomotives. Fewer attacks have been carried out on Luftwaffe ground organization than during the previous week. Supplies for agents continues at the same level. Active enemy air reconnaissance has been carried out in the Dunkirk-Dieppe sector, in the Flers-Caen-Isigny area, and also on the northern and western coasts of Brittany.

Whereas attacks on bridges have led to destruction or serious damage to all crossings over the Seine between Paris and Rouen, damage inflicted on coastal defenses is comparatively small.

Air reconnaissance has been carried out in the area of "Landgraf" divisions.

(d) Internal situation

Population in state of expectant tension and reserved as before. French Resistance organizations presumably ready for action again.

III In detail:

Northern Military District:

A. *Coastal defenses (Alterations):*

(a) Construction of Atlantic Wall:

Fortifications completed	1,226, 46 reinforced with concrete.
Approximate percentage of the whole project completed	68%
Progress of construction and particular defects	8 positions ready for action, 5 positions reinforced with concrete, 55 under construction.

Labor employed	(a) Soldiers: Unchanged
	(b) Civilians: Unchanged

(b) Consolidation of the land front: Further consolidation.

C. Operations of enemy aircraft:

(1) Number of raids:

Bombing raids	8 (27)
Strafing raids	82 (28)
Focal point of attacks	Through lines to Germany.

Total of attacks directed against:

Positions	3 (3)
Building sites	0 (0)
Transport targets	73 (26)
Airfields	9 (11)

(2) Casualties:

Soldiers killed	5 (1)
Soldiers wounded	7 (5)
German civilians killed	0 (0)
German civilians wounded	4 (0)
French civilians killed	116 (13)
French civilians injured	345 (29)

(3) Losses in material:

In attacks on positions	1 field wireless damaged.
In attacks on buildings under construction	
In attacks on transport targets	Buildings and track damaged at Roosendaal station, 51 locomotives, 5 electrical-driven cars, 22 passenger carriages and goods wagons damaged, 3 petrol wagons burnt out,

	14 barges and 1 2 cm. anti-aircraft gun damaged.
Unserviceable airfields	0 (0)
In attacks on airfields	1 Me 109 (100%), 1 anti-aircraft installation damaged, buildings damaged.
In other attacks	2 factories, numerous houses damaged or destroyed.

(4) Aircraft losses:

Enemy	21
Own	4

D.

(1) Feeling and behavior of the civilian population: Unchanged.

(2) Instances of sabotage:

Against railways	1
Against cables	1
Against crops	0
Against soldiers	0
Attacks with use of explosives	0
Cases of arson	0
Others	Terrorist attack on defense corps control post.

15th Army H.Q.:

A. Coastal defenses (Alterations):

(a) Organization of Defense: Flak Regiment 37 transferred to 348th Infantry Division, Flak Regiment 36 transferred to 344th Infantry Division.

The beach at St.-Aubin-sur-Mer looking west as it appeared in 1946. An anti-tank gun position can be seen at the top center of the photo. The Atlantic Wall consisted of fortifications installed mainly by the Todt organization and of many natural obstacles, such as the cliffs shown here. Wherever beaches were accessible to invasion, Rommel worked feverishly to have obstacles and mines installed for both low and high tide.

(b) Construction of Atlantic Wall:

Fortifications completed	17 pillboxes, 5 gun emplacements, 103 machine gun, anti-tank gun, and infantry positions, 1 anti-aircraft position, 1 battle H.Q., 3 artillery firing positions, 1 command post, dugouts for men and ammunition.
Approximate percentage of the whole project completed	62%
Progress of construction and particular defects	According to plan in general. Lack of timber, barbed wire, cement, sectional iron, hoop iron. Inadequate allocation of mines and wire. Continual breakdown of automatic sprayers impeding construction of coastal defenses.
Labor employed	(a) Soldiers: 29,889 (b) Civilians: 36,120 + 742 prisoners of war.

(c) Consolidation of the land front: Construction completed for field service. Machine gun positions, foxholes, mortar positions, 1 large minefield, dummy minefields, air land-ing obstacles, anti-tank and infantry positions, observation positions. Partial lack of cement, wire, mines, shells, hoop iron and workmen.

C. *Operations of enemy aircraft:*

(1) Number of raids:

Bombing raids	182 (190)
Strafing raids	109 (208)

Focal point of attacks	Bomber formations: Ostend–St. Omer–Amiens–Neufchatel–Le Treport, Fecamp, Le Havre, Rouen–Bernay, Evreux, Creil, Chartres, Brussels, Charleroi, Hasselt, Antwerp, Liege, Chauny, Douai. Reconnaissance: Dunkirk, Ghent-Bethune, Somme-Doullens-Amiens-Neufchatel-Dieppe. Fighter and fighter-bomber formations: Ghent-Mecheln-Charleroi-Laon-Compiegne-Conches-Honfleur.

Total of attacks directed against:

Positions	37 (53)
Building sites	62 (15)
Transport targets	139 (220)
Airfields	25 (69)

(2) Casualties:

Soldiers killed	387 (61)
Soldiers wounded	298 (156)
German civilians killed	2 (17)
German civilians wounded	— (35)
French civilians killed	74 (273)
French civilians injured	35 (641)

(3) Losses in material:

In attacks on positions	Destroyed: 2 Freya sets, 1 medium wave locator set, 1 searchlight-directing installation, 4 other Luftwaffe Signals installations, (several other installations—exact

number not known), 1 naval gun, 1 2 cm. gun, several huts and buildings, 2 M/T vehicles. Burnt out: 8,000 litres crude oil, ammunition and supply dumps.
Damaged: Several buildings and huts, several positions, 3 Luftwaffe Signals installations, 1 searchlight (60 cm.), 1 field generating set and special trailer for 2 cm. gun.
Buried: 2 guns (17 cm.), 2 tank guns (5 cm.), 2 2 cm. guns (out of commission for some time. Heavy personnel casualties (157 wounded, 226 dead and 102 missing) in an attack on Beverloo (16 km. North of Hasselt) on troop camps, permanent naval regiment, barracks of infantry camp and Burg Leopold. Damage to wires and cables.

In attacks on buildings under construction	Damaged: 9
In attacks on transport targets	Destroyed: 1 freight railway station, 6 works buildings, 6 works plants, 9 railway bridges, 47 locomotives, 416 railway cars, railway tracks. Damaged: 2 passenger railway stations, 12 works buildings, 2 works plants, 4 bridges, 1 water tower, 59 locomotives, 116 railway cars, heavy track damage. 1 bridge, 2 trucks destroyed, 2 road bridges damaged, 3 roads damaged, 2 dams, 5 ships damaged.

A Halifax bomber of No. 6 RCAF Group over France, July 1944. The Allied bombing campaign during the three months preceding D-Day was a significant part of the invasion preparations. Rail lines, engines, rolling stock, tunnels, bridges, airfields, and Atlantic Wall fortifications were bombed more heavily in the Pas de Calais than Normandy to advance the deception of Operation FORTITUDE. The bombing disrupted German troop movements, reinforcement, and supply lines during the invasion.

Unserviceable airfields	Maldeghem, Epinoy, Poix-Ost, Cambrai, Ursel.
In attacks on airfields	Destroyed: 1 aircraft, fuelling installation, 7 hangars, circuits. Damaged: 2 aircraft, 6 runways, 6 tarmacs, 1 workshop, 5 airfield buildings, 1 boundary lighting, 2 anti-aircraft positions, 4 anti-aircraft guns, telephone and electricity lines.

| In other attacks | Destroyed: 1 power station, large number of houses (exact figures not possible). Damaged: 2 factories, a large number of houses (exact figures not possible). |

(4) Aircraft losses:

Enemy	37 (29)
Own	— (3)

D.

(1) Feeling and behavior of the civilian population: Continues expectant and reserved; not hostile. Bad feeling in LXXXII A.K. sector owing to harvest having been partially damaged by defense measures.

(2) Instances of sabotage:

Against railways	3
Against cables	2
Against crops	0
Against soldiers	2
Attacks with use of explosives	3
Cases of arson	1
Others	0

7th Army H.Q.:

A. *Coastal defenses (Alterations):*

(a) Organization of Defense: Unchanged.

(b) Construction of Atlantic Wall:

| Fortifications completed | 6 fortified buildings, 1 reinforced concrete fortified building. |

Approximate percentage of the whole project completed	18%
Progress of construction and particular defects	Working of 6,361 cubic metres of reinforced concrete. Completion of field constructions held up for the moment in favour of beach and air landing obstacles. Lack of cement and wire, accessories and wood, pillbox shutters and doors, inadequate flow of supplies, lack of fuel, poor transport situation, shortage of trucks hinders ongoing construction. Cement: 200 instead of 1600 railway cars. Wire quantities: 305 tonnes.
Labor employed	(a) Soldiers: 36,848 (b) Civilians: 62,745

(c) Consolidation of the land front: —

B. Enemy operations on the coast: —

C. Operations of enemy aircraft:

(1) Number of raids:

Bombing raids	72 (53)
Strafing raids	31 (35)
Focal point of attacks	Fortified positions, transportation targets.

Total of attacks directed against:

Positions	52 (32)
Building sites	— (3)
Transport targets	29 (33)
Airfields	7 (6)

(2) Casualties:

Soldiers killed	31 (26), 27 missing.
Soldiers wounded	125 (62)
German civilians killed	— (2)
German civilians wounded	3 (7)
French civilians killed	56 (4), 150 missing.
French civilians injured	190 (—)

(3) Losses in material:

In attacks on positions	Destroyed: 4 positions under construction, 3 field bunkers, 1 crew shelter, 2 barracks, 1 water tower.
In attacks on buildings under construction	—
In attacks on transport targets	49 locomotives and large quantities of freight material, heavy track damage.
Unserviceable airfields	—
In attacks on airfields	Destroyed: 3 hangars, 2 anti-aircraft gun positions, 2 motor cars, 3 trucks. Damaged: Tarmac, 4 aircraft, 3 motor cars, 2 trucks, 1 Luftwaffe installation.
In other attacks	1 ship and 1 motor boat damaged.

(4) Aircraft losses:

Enemy	16 (21)
Own	2 (0)

D.

(1) Feeling and behavior of the civilian population: Attitude of population unchanged. Railway sabotage in Boulogne increasing again.

(2) Instances of sabotage:

Against railways	5 (1)
Against cables	—
Against crops	—
Against soldiers	3 (8)
Attacks with use of explosives	2 (1)
Cases of arson	—
Others	—

G.H.Q., XXXXVII Panzer Corps:

C. Operations of enemy aircraft:

(1) Number of raids:

Bombing raids	4
Strafing raids	Continual.
Focal point of attacks	Seine bridge, Gaillon

Total of attacks directed against:

Positions	—
Building sites	—
Transport targets	4
Airfields	—

(2) Casualties:

Soldiers killed	—
Soldiers wounded	4
German civilians killed	—
German civilians wounded	—
French civilians killed	Not known.
French civilians injured	Not known.

(3) Losses in material:

In attacks on positions	—

In attacks on buildings under construction	—
In attacks on transport targets	Seine bridge, Coucelles sur Seine destroyed.
Unserviceable airfields	—
In attacks on airfields	—
In other attacks	—

CHAPTER 2

From the Normandy Landings to the Surrender of Cherbourg, June 6–July 2, 1944

While the final preparations were underway for Operation OVERLORD, it was business as usual in Germany and occupied Europe. The German Air Force High Command sent out a message instructing the First Parachute Army at Nancy to conserve consumption of aircraft fuel as much as possible. Supply of goods was to be made by rail to preserve fuel for training and production. Most senior officers in the Seventh Army were attending a series of war games at Rennes. There was great consternation upon learning of the fall of Rome on the Italian Front.[1]

Just before midnight on the evening of June 5, it was discovered that the BBC was broadcasting a large number of messages to the French Resistance. The Fifteenth Army in the Seine was alerted, but Speidel did not alert the Seventh Army in Normandy. As Allied paratroops landed in Normandy after midnight, feverish activity at von Rundstedt's headquarters tried to determine whether this signaled the start of the invasion or whether it was merely a diversion. At 3:00 A.M., General Witt of the 12th SS received a signal from 711th Division: "Enemy airborne landing behind our left wing." By 4:00 A.M., von Rundstedt had decided that the landings must be dealt with. At dawn, an armada of over six thousand ships put the Allied invasion forces ashore along the coast of Normandy,

---

[1] Hinsley, 308–11.

with landing craft, amphibious tanks, and special-purpose vehicles touching-down on five beaches, code-named Utah and Omaha in the American sector and Gold, Juno, and Sword in the British-Canadian sector. To counter the landings, von Rundstedt requested the release of the panzer reserve from OKW and was enraged by the refusal.[2] Hitler was still sleeping and could not be disturbed.[3] Keitel was also asleep. Jodl awoke at 6:00 A.M. but was still not convinced that this was the main invasion. A second landing could still come at the Seine. As a result, of the available armored divisions, only the 21st Panzer went into action on June 6, yet even its commanding officer had not received orders to do so. On his own initiative, Lieutenant General Feuchtinger ordered the 21st Panzer Division forward at 7:30 A.M. after the men had already waited five hours beside their tanks.[4] Upon moving forward, they found the British in control of the only bridge across the Orne River north of Caen. To get across the river, they were forced to go around the long way through Caen and it was mid-afternoon before Feuchtinger's panzers were able to mount an attack against the British advance.[5]

Three German infantry divisions, the 709th, 716th, and 352nd, underwent a massive air and sea bombardment and then bore the brunt of an attack by elements of eight Allied divisions without any support from their higher headquarters. Von Rundstedt finally obtained the release of I SS Panzer Corps at 4:00 P.M., but the main body of that formation took two days to reach the invasion area as a result of air attacks and broken bridges. Göring's Luftwaffe could only launch 319 sorties against the 12,015 mounted by the Allies, and the Germans were unable to shoot down a single Allied plane.[6] On Omaha Beach, however, the well-trained and resolute 352nd Infantry inflicted heavy casualties on the Americans. Upon

---

[2] Stacey, 122; D'Este, 118.

[3] Stacey, 122.

[4] Russell Weigley, *Eisenhower's Lieutenants: The Campaign of France and Germany, 1944–1945* (Indianapolis: Indiana University Press, 1990), 128.

[5] Stacey, 124.

[6] Keegan, 143.

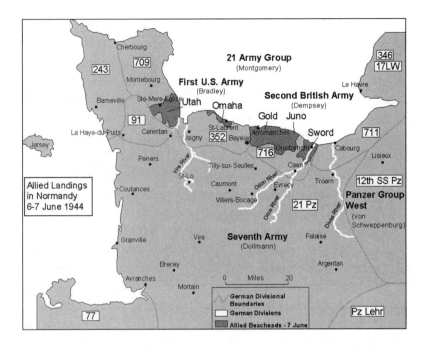

receiving news of the invasion, Rommel drove back to France, arriving at 10:30 P.M. with orders from Hitler to "drive the invaders back into the sea by midnight." Rommel was dissatisfied with Feuchtinger's performance, particularly with the small number of gliders that had been shot down. Feuchtinger, for his part, complained that prior to Rommel's return he had received no orders and had been forbidden to move without them.[7]

By June 7, the Allied landings had established a tenuous fifty-mile front, although in some places the bridgeheads were less than a mile deep. The Atlantic Wall turned out to be a less formidable obstacle than originally feared, with the beach obstacles being cleared in a matter of hours thanks to careful Allied preparation and reconnaissance. Yet the outcome of the Battle of Normandy still hung in the balance and would be determined by the ability of either side to build up enough reserves within or against the bridgehead. Should von Rundstedt prove successful in redeploying his full forces to Nor-

---

[7] D'Este, 126, 138.

mandy, the eight Allied divisions now ashore could be over-
whelmed. Due to the success of Operation FORTITUDE, however, twenty divisions of the Fifteenth Army remained tied
down in the Pas de Calais for another two months, awaiting a
second Allied invasion there.[8] That left the fifteen divisions of
Seventh Army to drive the Allies back into the sea before they
could consolidate their hold over the bridgehead.

Overnight on June 7, the 12th SS "Hitler Youth" Panzer
Division entered the fray when it was brought forward to
oppose the Canadians outside Caen. In this sector, the German
711th and 716th Divisions had born the brunt of the British-
Canadian assault. Here, regrouping elements of shattered
units and reinforcements pressing forwards created an unsta-
ble perimeter to contain the invasion beachhead. Further west,
as men and vehicles continued to pour ashore from the sea,
the Americans consolidated their positions around Utah and
Omaha, and on the morning of June 8, the U.S. First Army
established contact with the British Second Army when the two
formations linked up near Port-en-Bessin.

On June 10, Rommel wrote of traffic being pinned down
and troop movements paralyzed while the enemy was able to
maneuver freely. He was unable to get fuel or ammunition to
his troops. Rommel wished to concentrate his forces against
the American bridgehead near Carentan, but Hitler vetoed
this, ordering him instead to attack the British outside Caen.
Here, Rommel succeeded in concentrating four panzer divisions against the British and Canadians, with the 21st Panzer,
12th SS Panzer, Panzer Lehr and 2nd Panzer swinging into line
to prevent Montgomery from seizing his D-Day objectives. By
this time, the Allies had more than doubled their number of
troops and vehicles in the bridgehead. They also achieved a significant success on June 11 as ULTRA intelligence pinpointed
the location of Panzer Group West headquarters at La Caine.
The aerial bombardment that followed receipt of this information was so severe that Geyr von Schweppenburg was wounded

---

[8] Ziemke, "Rundstedt," in Barnett, ed., 200.

and seventeen of his staff officers killed.[9] As a result, the German counterattack planned for the next day had to be delayed by twenty-four hours.

Further Allied successes came with the link-up of Omaha and Utah beaches in the American sector, thereby establishing a continuous Allied front along the fifty-mile perimeter. The bridgehead was now firmly established, but Montgomery was still denied entry to Caen, his goal for the first day of battle. Rommel's four panzer divisions had pinned down the British and Canadian forces, but did not yet have sufficient infantry or armored strength to dislodge them. To the west, the Americans captured Carentan and began fighting their way across the Cotentin to Cherbourg. Here they faced less formidable opposition but more difficult terrain than did the British and Canadians.

On June 17, Hitler flew to the Western Front for a meeting with Field Marshals von Rundstedt and Rommel at Margival near Soissons to discuss the enemy's plans for breaking through the perilously thin ring of German defenses. Hitler still believed that the main Allied assault was yet to come from the Pas de Calais area and the Fifteenth Army should be held in readiness there. The Führer rejected requests from Rommel and von Rundstedt to withdraw their forces back beyond the range of naval gunfire in order to consolidate German lines. He insisted on a rigid defense of every inch of ground.[10]

That same day, American tanks had cut off the Cotentin Peninsula, isolating the city of Cherbourg and the German forces stationed there.[11] Hitler's response was that the defenders were to stand fast; "Fortress Cherbourg" was to be held at all costs. Meanwhile, the Great Channel Storm that started on June 16 grew in intensity, reaching its peak three days later. On June 19, hurricane-force winds completely destroyed the American artificial "Mulberry" harbor at St. Laurent and badly

---

[9] Terry Copp, *Fields of Fire: The Canadians in Normandy* (Toronto: University of Toronto Press, 2003), 75; D'Este, 167.

[10] Hinsley, 175; D'Este, 152.

[11] OKW, 41.

damaged the British Mulberry at Arromanches. Once the storm ended, eight hundred vessels of all sizes were stranded, damaged or destroyed[12] and the "Gooseberry" breakwaters that formed a component of the harbors had broken open to the sea. The unloading of reinforcements, vehicles, supplies, ammunition, and artillery was badly delayed, rendering the capture of Cherbourg and its vital port facilities now even more essential to the Americans.

The bad weather, interfering with Allied air attacks, allowed Rommel to reinforce his Normandy defenses with an additional four armored divisions: Hausser's II Panzer Corps (9th SS and 10th SS Panzer Divisions) from Poland, 1st SS Panzer Division from the north, and 2nd SS Panzer Division from southern France.[13] The Germans now intended to mass their tanks for a powerful strike in the Caen sector at the same time that Montgomery was readying his next attempt to break through their defenses in that sector. Code-named Operation EPSOM, Montgomery's third attempt to capture or encircle Caen had been postponed to June 26 owing to bad weather and the seasickness of newly-arrived troops.[14] Intended to be a major offensive across the Odon River, Operation EPSOM aimed at seizing the high ground dominating the west bank of the Orne southwest of Caen.

Bad news began to flow into German headquarters from all sides. On June 22, the Red Army's overwhelming summer offensive opened on the third anniversary of Hitler's 1941 invasion of the Soviet Union. This was in accordance with Stalin's agreement at Teheran in 1943 to launch an offensive that would prevent the Germans from transferring additional forces to France once the second front had been opened. Within two days, Germany's Army Group Center was in full retreat before the tide of Soviet forces. In the west, it took the 2nd SS Panzer Division seventeen days following the invasion

---

[12] Copp, 80.
[13] D'Este, 233.
[14] Stacey, 145.

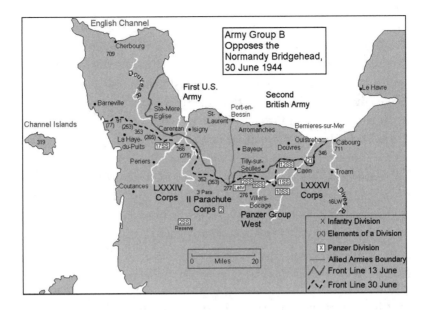

to move from its base in Toulouse to Normandy.[15] The trip should have taken three days, but the successful destruction of all bridges on the Loire between Orléans and the sea, repeated acts of sabotage by French resistance fighters under British agents, ambushes, air attacks, and lack of fuel caused extensive delays.[16]

On 25 June, OKW learned that American troops had stormed into the suburbs of Cherbourg. Lieutenant General Karl von Schlieben, the commander of the fortress-city, appealed to Rommel for permission to surrender. Two thousand of his men from the 709th Infantry Division were wounded and could not be treated. Rommel replied that in accordance with the Führer's orders he was to hold out to the last round.[17] Meanwhile, Allied warships waiting offshore began pounding the city with their guns, just as Rommel and von Rundstedt had warned Hitler at their meeting of June 17. On the evening of June 26, despite stubborn resistance on the

---

[15] Gilbert, 543.

[16] D'Este, 233.

[17] Keegan, 160.

part of the defenders, Cherbourg fell to the U.S. 9th Infantry Division. In spite of Hitler's admonition to "continue to fight to the last cartridge," von Schlieben surrendered what was left of the Fort du Roule garrison, the last point of German resistance on the peninsula. Hitler was furious; he summoned von Rundstedt and Rommel to Berchtesgaden for a meeting on June 29 to discuss the lack of progress in the West and the fall of Cherbourg.[18]

Added to his troubles, written in von Rundstedt's weekly situation report, was his worry that FUSAG in Britain was ready to embark. He believed the force was even larger than Montgomery's 21st Army Group already facing him in Normandy. Three-quarters of a million Allied troops were already ashore. The Americans had almost complete control over Cherbourg and had begun their advance toward St. Lô. Now von Rundstedt had to justify the course of the battle to Hitler. At Berchtesgaden, Hitler was intransigent and refused to accept the opinions of his field marshals that the existing battle lines were untenable.[19] He reluctantly agreed to abandon his plans for a major offensive to split the Allied armies and retake the port of Cherbourg, but refused the massive reinforcements, anti-aircraft guns, and aircraft that his field commanders insisted were necessary. Two days later, von Rundstedt asked for permission from OKW to begin planned withdrawals to a new line six miles south of Caen and beyond the effective range of naval artillery. Hitler denied the request: the present positions were to be held and any further enemy breakthrough must be prevented by obstinate defense or immediate counterattacks. It was at this point that OKW Chief of Staff, Field Marshal Keitel, plaintively asked von Rundstedt, "What shall we do?" In response, von Rundstedt is reported to have burst out, shouting, "Make peace you idiots! What else can you do?"[20] The

---

[18] Stacey, 149; Hastings, 175.

[19] Martin Blumenson, *Breakout and Pursuit*, United States Army in World War II Series: The European Theater of Operations (Washington, DC: Center of Military History, United States Army, 1989), 26.

[20] Stacey, 149.

next day, July 2, 1944, von Rundstedt received notification that he was being replaced as Commander-in-Chief West by Field Marshal von Kluge.[21]

✠

ESTIMATE OF THE SITUATION ON JUNE 11, 1944

The course of the fighting in Normandy so far clearly shows that the objectives of the enemy are:

(1) To establish a deep bridgehead between the Orne and the Vire as a base for a later attack with strong forces into central France, probably in the direction of Paris.

(2) To cut off the Cotentin peninsula and to take Cherbourg as quickly as possible, in order to gain a large and serviceable harbor. It seems possible, however, as the situation is developing, that the enemy may abandon the occupation of the Cotentin peninsula if fighting becomes too hard there, and make an early thrust into the interior of France, throwing in all of his resources.

Owing to the obstinate resistance of troops in the coastal defense sectors and the counter-attacks immediately undertaken by the major reserves available, the course of enemy operations has, in spite of the employment of most powerful means of warfare, taken appreciably longer than our adversary had hoped. The enemy also appears to be using more forces than originally intended.

The enemy is visibly reinforcing on land, under the cover of very strong aircraft formations. The Luftwaffe and our navy are not in a position to offer him appreciable opposition, especially by day. Thus the strength of the enemy on land is increasing more quickly than our reserves can reach the front.

Owing to the enemy's overwhelming air superiority it was not possible to bring up the 1st SS Panzer Corps, the 7th Mor-

---

[21] OKW, 52.

tar Brigade, III Flak Corps and II Paratroop Corps (Meindl) quickly into the area between the Orne and the Vire, or to make a counter-attack on the enemy forces which had landed. The 7th Mortar Brigade, III Flak Corps and II Paratroop Corps (Meindl) are still on the way up to the front, the 1st SS Panzer Corps has been forced on to the defensive in hard fighting and is being attacked on its open left flank by superior armored formations.

The Army Group must content itself for the present with forming a cohesive front between the Orne and the Vire with the forces which are gradually coming up, and allowing the enemy to advance. In these circumstances it is unfortunately not possible to relieve troops still resisting in many coastal positions. The Army Group is trying to replace the panzer formations in action with infantry divisions as soon as possible, and to form mobile reserves with them.

In the next few days the Army Group intends to remove the centre of its operations to the Carentan-Montebourg area, in order to annihilate the enemy there and to divert the danger threatening Cherbourg. Only when this has been successfully accomplished can the enemy between the Orne and the Vire be attacked. Unfortunately this operation can no longer be supported by our fighter formations, as there are no longer any airfields near the front at our disposal.

Our operations in Normandy will be rendered exceptionally difficult, and even partially impossible, by the following conditions:

(a) the extraordinarily strong, and in some respects overwhelming superiority of the enemy Air Force.

As I personally and officers of my staff have repeatedly proved, and as unit commanders, especially Obergruppenführer Sepp Dietrich, report, the enemy has complete control of the air over the battle area and up to 100 km. behind the front. Almost all transport on roads, byroads and on open country is prevented by day by strong fighter-bomber and bomber formations. Movements of our troops in the battle area by day are almost completely prevented, while the enemy

Looking out from a German gun position at Bernières-sur-Mer on June 6, 1944. Allied landing craft can be seen offshore. On D-Day German troops faced constant naval and aerial bombardment. Because of shortages of pilots and fuel, however, the Luftwaffe was unable to match the 12,015 Allied sorties, launching only 319 of their own.

can operate freely. In rear areas all confined areas are continually exposed to attacks, and it is very difficult to bring up the necessary supplies of ammunition and fuel to the troops.

Even the movements of smaller formations, artillery taking up position, deployment of tanks and so on, are immediately bombarded from the air with annihilating effect. Troops and staffs are forced to hide in terrain which provides cover during the day, in order to escape these continual attacks from the air.

On June 9 in the battle area of the SS Corps, numerous enemy fighter-bomber formations circled uninterruptedly over the battlefield and strong bomber formations bombarded troops, villages, bridges, and road junctions as heavily as possible without consideration for the population. Neither our flak nor the Luftwaffe seems to be in a position to check this crippling and destructive operation of the enemy Air Force (27,000 sorties in one day). The army and SS troops are defending themselves as well as they can with the means at their disposal, but ammunition is scarce and can be replaced only under the most difficult conditions.

(b) The effect of heavy naval artillery.

Up to 640 heavy calibre guns were used. The effect is so strong that operation with infantry or panzer formations in the area commanded by this quick-firing artillery is not possible. In spite of this heavy fire garrisons on the coast and the troops sent to counter-attack in the area of Montebourg have held their positions with the utmost tenacity. It must be expected, however, that the enemy warships will intervene further in the fighting on land, especially in the Cotentin peninsula, if the Luftwaffe and our navy do not succeed in destroying them.

(c) The material equipment of the Anglo-Americans with numerous new weapons and war materials is far superior to the equipment of our divisions. As Obergruppenführer Sepp Dietrich informed me, enemy armored formations carry on the battle at a range of up to 3,500 meters with maximum expenditure of ammunition and splendidly supported by the enemy Air Force. This was also the case at Alamein. Furthermore, their great superiority in artillery and extremely large supplies of ammunition are increasingly apparent.

(d) Parachute and airborne troops are used in such large numbers and so effectively, that the troops attacked have a difficult task in defending themselves. If enemy airborne forces land in a territory unoccupied by us, they immediately make themselves ready for defense and can be defeated only with difficulty by infantry attacks with artillery support. Further operations of this type, especially in areas not occupied by our troops, must be expected. The Luftwaffe has unfortunately not been able to take action against these formations as was originally planned. Since the enemy can cripple our mobile formations with his Air Force by day, while he operates with fast moving forces and airborne troops, our position is becoming extraordinarily difficult.

I request that the Fuehrer be informed of this.

Rommel
June 12, 1944

WEEKLY REPORT, JUNE 12–19, 1944

I Estimate of the situation as a whole:

The enemy has brought about 25 divisions and a large number of H.Q. troops of all types into Normandy, and has formed them up into one bridgehead from the Orne to Montebourg. He has carried out his plan to cut off the northern part of the Cotentin peninsula, in order to take possession of Cherbourg. Between the Orne and the Vire the enemy, with 2 noticeable concentrations, continued his attempts to create a jumping-off base for the attack into the French interior, especially in the direction of Paris.

(a) between Tilly sur Seulles and Caumont,

(b) on both sides of Route Nationale 172 to take possession of the St. Lo area.

Despite his great superiority, especially in air power and naval artillery, the enemy has gained no successes in repeated large scale attacks with ruthless employment of men and material, and has even lost ground in the Caumont area.

The slowly progressing mopping-up operation between the Dives and the Orne has suffered losses from the fire of naval artillery and the operations of the enemy Air Force. According to intelligence and reliable captured documents the enemy has reached none of his distant objectives, but has been forced to employ far greater forces than was originally planned.

It must be expected that the enemy will bring up new forces,—2 British army corps have already been identified— and will prepare a general offensive between Tilly sur Seulles

The Canadian 9th Infantry Brigade comes ashore at Bernières-sur-Mer on the afternoon of June 6, shortly after the beachhead was secured. The soldiers are disembarking from LCI 299 (Landing Craft, Infantry) using ramps built by engineers. By evening they would be in the line of fire advancing toward their divisional objective at Carpiquet.

and St. Lo in a southerly or south-south-easterly direction, with concentration of forces, and after extensive preparation by the Air Force and artillery of all types. At the same time the 1st American Army, covered in the south, will prepare for the attack on Cherbourg, in order to gain the port, which is of decisive importance to the enemy.

In front of the 15th Army sector the focal points of air attack appeared clearly again as the Channel front on both sides of Cap Gris Nez and on both sides of the Somme. According to enemy regrouping and strategic and technical opportunities, a large-scale enemy landing on the Channel front on both sides of Cap Gris Nez or between the Somme and Le Havre must be expected. The general offensive out of the Normandy bridgehead and a new large-scale landing may be made simultaneously, both having the Paris area as the objective.

The enemy has suffered severe casualties in the battles in the bridgehead and has so far lost more than 500 armored vehicles and over 1,000 aircraft.

An estimate of the effect of the long-range weapon is not possible at present, owing to the short time in which it has been used and to the lack of reliable data.

Internal Situation

The population is friendly in the theater of operations, and sabotage and other resistance activities which broke out again in the first days of the invasion have decreased noticeably.

Details will be submitted after receipt of reports from the armies.

Rommel,
Field Marshal

WEEKLY REPORT, JUNE 19–26, 1944

I Estimate of the situation as a whole:

The battle for the fortress of Cherbourg has been the main feature of the weekly report. After the enemy cut off the Cotentin peninsula on June 18, and our own troops, according to orders, had to make a costly retreat to Cherbourg, the enemy attempted to force the capture of Cherbourg by encirclement from the west, employing his superior forces, which included 5 infantry divisions, 1 armored division, and many H.Q. troops. On June 21 he succeeded in reaching the 50 km. long Cherbourg land front practically at the same time as the retreating von Schlieben battle group.

After a brief interval for preparation, during which constant air attacks were made and greatly superior artillery was brought up, the enemy drove 4 wedges into the outer defense ring on June 23. The unequal heroic struggle of the gallant defenders of Cherbourg continued without any possibility of ground, air or naval support until the evening of June 25, while the enemy with the superior equipment of his three services systematically reduced the garrison. At present a few pockets of resistance are still holding out in the city area of Cherbourg and on the Jobourg peninsula.

This has proved that such an extensive fortress cannot be held without sufficient troops and without air and naval support. The fortresses are not equal to the massed enemy Air Force and naval artillery, without corresponding counter-action on our part. Even the strongest fortifications were demolished piece by piece.

The other two local enemy concentrations were on both sides of Tilly sur Seulles and in the St. Lo–Carentan area. While the defensive success of June 17 resulted in a slackening of the enemy offensive in the latter area, an attack was made on both sides of Tilly sur Seulles on June 25; after intensive bombardment from land and air on a 7 km. front, the enemy succeeding in breaking through to a depth of 5 km.

Once again the enemy suffered heavy losses in these battles—as he himself admits—including more than 750 armored vehicles since June 6. Our own losses are however also extraordinarily high. Exclusive of the Cherbourg garrison, the following casualties were suffered from June 6 until June 25:

897	officers (including 6 generals, 63 C.O.'s and 4 officers of the General Staff)
40,217	N.C.O.'s and men
1,956	Eastern members
——	
43,070	

Heavy losses, especially in panzer divisions, and lack of replacements are causing great anxiety owing to the large decrease in strength caused by the daily bombardment from land and naval artillery and from the air.

Enemy operational plans are judged to be as follows. The enemy has sent 27–31 divisions and a large number of H.Q. troops into the bridgehead and further reinforcements are to be expected. In England another 67 large formations are ready,

This gun position formed part of a strongpoint at St.-Aubin-sur-Mer, including on 50mm anti-tank gun and several machine guns. Earlier naval bombardment had failed to destroy the resistance nest and its 100 defenders of the 716th Infantry Division. This gun was eventually suppressed by the Canadian North Shore (New Brunswick) Regiment. By the evening of June 6, the 716th had suffered 80 percent casualties. U.S. AIR FORCE

of which at least 57 could be used for a large-scale operation. Enemy distribution of forces in the bridgehead, naval movements, intercepted radio orders to reconnoitre the Touques and Risle sectors and other intelligence reports indicate a thrust in the area to the north and north-west of Caen in the direction of Paris.

This thrust could be linked up with a large-scale landing between the Somme and Le Havre, and this is indicated by agent's reports and increased enemy air reconnaissance. The effect of the long-range weapons may also compel the enemy to make a landing in this area. The combined objective of both these operations will be the area around Paris, whose rail communication to the east was completely cut off by the enemy Air Force on June 25.

After the release of enemy forces in the Cherbourg area for other operations the enemy may regroup to the south and after about June 30 may attack between Carentan and Portbail towards the south, in order to gain possession of the line St. Lo–Coutances and thus secure the necessary road communications from Cherbourg harbour to the eastern part of the landing area.

The increasing supply crisis at the battle front deserves special attention. Owing to lack of space, the breakdown of the railway system, and incessant enemy air attacks, it is impossible at present to guarantee a regular flow of supplies for our own operations.

In Detail:

Situation at sea

(1) Enemy activity in the landing area
Large-scale use of battleships, cruisers and destroyers for coastal bombardment, especially off the Orne estuary. Increased patrol of sea areas off Cherbourg, the Channel Islands, and the northern coast of Brittany by groups of cruisers and destroyers, concentrated in the area between Ile de Batz and Les Sept Iles.

(2) Enemy minelaying activity
No recognizable area of concentration.

Situation in the air
Fighter, fighter-bomber, and close combat formations concentrated on the support of ground troops in the battle area—especially around Cherbourg—and in rear areas, while heavy bomber formations concentrated on special buildings. The enemy's great superiority also allowed him to continue attacks on airfields and transport targets.

While only isolated attacks were made in the Northern Military District, the V-1 launching sites in northern France and Belgium were attacked incessantly. During the day 4-engined aircraft made up to 1,450 sorties, twin-engined aircraft 300. Attacks against Luftwaffe ground organization and railway installations caused considerable damage in some instances. Increased air reconnaissance was carried out on both sides of Dieppe and in the area between Fecamp and Etretat.

Regular fighter sorties up to the line Paris-Rennes caused an almost complete stoppage of road transport during the day. Owing to very strong fighter defense urgently required, support for Cherbourg and air reconnaissance of the Caen-Bayeux area was rendered impossible.

Considerably increased air attacks were carried out against our defense forces in the whole Channel area by day and night. Our sea transport can only operate in special weather conditions which exclude the possibility of fighter-bomber attack. Air attacks were continued against ports on the mainland and islands in the Channel Island area. Continuous fighter-bomber attacks were made against naval radar stations in Brittany.

Internal situation

Those sections of the population affected continue to feel embittered at the ruthless Anglo-American methods of warfare, especially with regard to air force operations, otherwise the majority of the population is reserved.

Inhabitants of the Belgian coast demand evacuation. The launching of the new weapon in the struggle against England aroused interest, and in some instances, satisfaction. Terrorist and sabotage operations are continually sustained by reinforcements of men and material from outside.

In the entire area of the Army Group the number of young men, alone or in groups, on the roads has further increased, so that there are grounds for suspicion of extensive recruiting for Resistance organizations. According to counter-intelligence reports, especially large numbers are arriving in the Cambrai area.

In Belgium and in the border area between Belgium and France the signs of a systematic Resistance organization under energetic leadership are increasing: former members of the

Looking east, remains of the battle at St.-Aubin-sur-Mer can be seen on the beach: a U.S. Army Air Force Thunderbolt that made an emergency landing, a duplex-drive tank put out of action during the landing, and a beached craft in the background. U.S. AIR FORCE

Wehrmacht are being recruited by call-up notices, and a supply organization is being built up. The number of acts of sabotage is increasing.

In Brittany continual reinforcement with well-trained, well-equipped men and experienced leaders (partly French parachute troops trained in England) by air and probably by sea has led to the formation of powerful fighting groups. Concentrations in areas Callae, to the north of Vannes, and in the more remote surroundings of Pontivy and Guincamp.

Northern Military District:

A. Coastal defenses (Alterations):

(a) Organization of Defense: Defense organization considerably weakened by withdrawal of 16th Luftwaffe Field Division.

(b) Construction of Atlantic Wall:

Fortifications completed	1,253 emplacements ready for action, 55 reinforced with concrete.
Approximate percentage of the whole project completed	Of previous construction programmes and plans up to August 30, 1944, 69% completed, 1% reinforced with concrete.
Progress of construction and particular defects	6 positions ready for action, 13 reinforced with concrete.
Labor employed	About 17,000 in fortress type and about 46,000 in field type construction.

B. Enemy operations on the coast:
None.

C. Operations of enemy aircraft:

(1) Number of raids:

Bombing raids	7 (10)
Strafing raids	21 (11)
Focal point of attacks	Not known.

Total of attacks directed against:

Positions	2 (0)
Building sites	0 (0)
Transport targets	18 (6)

(2) Casualties:

Soldiers killed	8 (2)
Soldiers wounded	24 (8)
German civilians killed	0 (0)
German civilians wounded	0 (0)
French civilians killed	24 (15)
French civilians injured	51 (23)

(3) Losses in material:

In attacks on positions	1 locomotive destroyed, 1 damaged, 1 motor boat damaged.
In attacks on transport targets	16 locomotives out of commission, 6 railway cars damaged.
Unserviceable airfields	0
In attacks on airfields	Damage to buildings and tarmacs, several aircraft damaged.
In other attacks	1 farm and 3 houses destroyed, 9 houses damaged, blast furnace plant put out of action temporarily owing to the destruction of current and water supplies.

(4) Aircraft losses:

| Enemy | 33 (29) |
| Own | 5 (10) |

D.

(2) Instances of sabotage:

Against railways	1
Against cables	1
Against crops	0
Against soldiers	1
Attacks with use of explosives	1
Cases of arson	0

15th Army H.Q.:

A. Coastal defenses (Alterations):

(a) Organization of Defense: Defense organization weakened by withdrawal of 1st SS Panzer Division 'Adolf Hitler Bodyguard'. Reinforcement of threatened area of Le Havre by 89th Infantry Division seems urgently necessary.

(b) Construction of Atlantic Wall:

Fortifications completed	3 pillboxes, 4 gun emplacements, 5 anti-aircraft positions, 4 anti-tank gun positions, 2 dugouts (fortress type), infantry, artillery, anti-aircraft, anti-tank gun, machine gun and mortar positions, observation positions, firing positions, dugouts for men, equipment, ammunition and fuel, 2 minefields extended, beach defenses, 60 tons of mines moved, 95 km. minebelt, air landing stakes provided with mines and explosives.
Approximate percentage of the whole project completed	48%
Progress of construction and particular defects	Considerably restricted by alarm conditions, transport conditions, breakdown of current, lack of material, building material, cement, sawn wood, fuel, anti-personnel and anti-tank mines, lack of labor.

Flanked on either side by steep cliffs, this German gun battery at
Longues-sur-Mer defended against the invasion by engaging in duels
with U.S. and British warships, but German gun emplacements on
the channel lacked fire-control systems to engage moving ships. The
cruiser HMS *Ajax* silenced the battery after firing 114 shells from its
six-inch guns. The Longues battery, captured by the British 50th
Infantry Division on June 7, included three large bunkers that still
contain their original 150mm guns.

Labor employed	(a) Soldiers: 19,576
	(b) Civilians: 18,528 +
	742 POWs.

(c) Consolidation of the land front: ./.

C. Operations of enemy aircraft:

(1) Number of raids:

Bombing raids	174 (95)
Strafing raids	31 (35)
Focal point of attacks	Bomber formations: Brussels–Hasselt–Laon–St. Quentin–Amiens–Aumale–Abbeville–Arras–Lens–Armentieres–St. Omer. Reconnaissance: Dunkirk–Bruges–Antwerp–St. Quentin–Arras–Amiens–Le Treport. Fighter-bombers and fighters: Ostend–Tournai–Fourmieres–Soissons–Beauvais–Fecamp.

Total of attacks directed against:

Positions	9 (3)
Building sites	79 (6)
Transport targets	75 (47)
Airfields	24 (58)

(2) Casualties:

Soldiers killed	201 (44)
Soldiers wounded	361 (104)
German civilians killed	1 (9)
German civilians wounded	— (6)
French civilians killed	41 (31)
French civilians injured	77 (52)

(3) Losses in material:

In attacks on positions	Destroyed: Luftwaffe Signals plotting station, 1 auxiliary aerial, 2 guns (3.7 cm.).

The bunkers of Courseulles-sur-Mer can be seen in the background of this photo taken in 1946. The Courseulles strongpoint included a 75mm gun, 88mm gun, and three 50mm anti-aircraft guns, in addition to 12,000–14,000 mines that had been laid on the beach between Courseulles and Bernières, a distance of about two miles.

	Damaged: 1 Luftwaffe Signals installation, 1 billet, 1 aircraft field generating set, tracks, 1 hangar, huts and circuits.
In attacks on buildings under construction	Destroyed: 1 Heavily damaged: 4 Slightly damaged: 9
In attacks on transport targets	Destroyed: 3 works buildings, 28 locomotives, 84 railway cars, 64 M/T vehicles, 3 trucks, a large number of railway installations. Damaged: 6 works buildings, 5 works plants, 4 railway bridges, 10 locomotives, 57 railway cars, 5 M/T vehicles, 2 guns (10.5 cm.), railway installations, telephone and electricity cables and 4 roads. Also 2 torpedo boats, 1 patrol vessel, 1 motor minesweeper and 2 barges sunk, 2 harbor

	installations, 1 lock, 2 torpedo boats, 1 minelayer, 1 motor minesweeper and 6 barges in part badly damaged.
Unserviceable airfields	Juvincourt (Amy, Melsebroeck, Abbeville, Drucat)
In attacks on airfields	Destroyed: 3 aircraft, 1 hangar, 3 airfield buildings, 3 huts and 300 litres aircraft fuel (89 octane). Damaged: 1 aircraft, 7 runways, 8 tarmacs, 1 aircraft bay, 2 hangars, 14 airfield buildings, 2 boundary lighting systems, 7 huts, 3 supply routes, water mains, electricity and telephone cables.
In other attacks	Destroyed: 1 rolling mill, 2 plants, 1 electricity works, a large number of houses. Damaged: A large number of houses, electricity cables and water mains.

(4) Aircraft losses:

Enemy	78
Own	17

D.

(2) Instances of sabotage:

Against railways	1
Against cables	1
Against soldiers	1

7th Army H.Q.:

A. Coastal defenses (Alterations):

(b) Construction of Atlantic Wall:

Fortifications completed	6 fortress type constructions, 1 field type construction reinforced with concrete.
Approximate percentage of the whole project completed	64,683 cubic meters of reinforced concrete from the Normandy summer program used.
Progress of construction and particular defects	6070 cubic meters of reinforced concrete during the week covered by the report. Construction of field-type defenses held up by A-plan and lack of sappers. Concentrated work on coastal defenses and air landing obstacles. Lack of cement, lumber, fuel, and transportation of every sort.
Labor employed	On the coastal front: (a) Soldiers 6,069 (b) Civilians 8,105 On the land front: (a) Soldiers 10,723 (b) Civilians 14,615

(c) Consolidation of the land front:

(2) Aircraft losses:

Enemy	7
Own	Not known.

For the Army Group High Command,

The Chief of General Staff,
Speidel

WEEKLY REPORT, JUNE 27–JULY 2, 1944

I Estimate of the situation as a whole:

The most substantial event of the week was the large-scale enemy attack to take possession of the area around Caen, in order to win a base for further operations in the direction of Paris.

The enemy commenced the attack on June 25, with a bombardment from land, sea and air, sent in 5 infantry divisions, 1 armored division, 3 armored brigades, and a considerable number of H.Q. troops—especially artillery—and was able to force a breakthrough 9 km. deep and 9 km. wide.

The breakthrough was held up at first by the heroic resistance of the 12th SS Panzer Division, the Panzer Training Division, units of the 1st SS Panzer Division the 2nd Panzer Division and the 2nd SS Panzer Division and was finally stopped by a well-timed counter attack by the II SS Panzer Corps which was supported by the concentrated fire of army artillery and 2 mortar brigades. In the course of the week the enemy suffered especially heavy casualties, losing more than 150 armored vehicles (amounting to more than 900 since the commencement of the invasion) and was no longer able to make a concentrated attack.

A continuation of our attempt to mop up the breakthrough area was repeatedly frustrated with heavy losses by day and night by the concentrated fire of the superior enemy naval and land artillery and of the Air Force. Our lack of artillery ammunition of all calibres made itself very noticeable.

After bringing up fresh forces (the enemy's reinforcements aggregate at least 2–3 divisions per week) and regrouping, a resumption of the attacks in the breakthrough area must be expected—various signs indicate an attack east of the Orne. The enemy objective is still a thrust at Caen.

While the heroic struggle of isolated pockets of resistance in Cherbourg ended on July 1 with the annihilation of the Keil battle group on the Jobourg peninsula, the enemy attempted to force a breakthrough in the St. Lo area with forces already brought down from Cherbourg, the main concentration of the

One of the main bunkers at Courseulles-sur-Mer, show on June 10, 1944. Rommel's strategy for defeating the invasion failed when the unclear chain of command, Rommel's absence, and Keitel's refusal to awaken Hitler on D-Day resulted in a series of delays. Only the 21st Panzer Division was able to engage the landing forces on June 6, and the deception of Operation FORTITUDE kept OKW convinced that the main thrust of the attack was yet to come in the Pas de Calais.

attack being on both sides of Villers Fossard. After severe battles lasting three days, the enemy was repulsed everywhere.

Reports of heavy enemy losses are piling up.

Our own losses from June 6 to July 1 amount to: —

1,137	officers (including 7 generals, 79 C.O.'s and 5 General Staff officers)
44,871	NCO's and men
1,095	Eastern Volunteers
47,103	

In addition

500	officers and officials
15,000	men (minimum figure, 17,500 according to a report from 7th Army H.Q.) of the Cherbourg garrison.

62,603	Total

Enemy strength and operational plans

At present in the landing area the enemy has approximately 33 divisions and strong H.Q. troops; in Great Britain another 64 large formations are standing by, 54 of which could be transferred to the mainland.

After the capture of the Caen area—by encirclement on two sides, if possible—and fresh consolidation, the enemy intends to commence the advance on Paris. At the same time he will attempt a concentrated attack on the St. Lo–Coutances area with forces released from the Cherbourg area totalling 10 infantry and 2 armored divisions, in an effort to consolidate his land base. Signs of this operation are apparent.

There are no fresh data concerning the objectives of the American 1st Army Group in Great Britain. A landing on both sides of the Somme as far as the Seine must be expected in view of strategic cooperation with the Montgomery Battle Group for the thrust on Paris and the elimination of the long range weapon.

A separate plan will follow regarding our plans.

II Situation at sea

Very heavy artillery fire from British, American and French battleships, cruisers and destroyers is concentrated on knocking out Cherbourg, covering landings off the Orne estuary, supporting the land battle at Caen, and silencing the coastal batteries.

Vessels are continually unloading along the invasion coast and active convoy movements are taking place in the Channel.

There are heavy shipping concentrations in the Thames and also at Harwich. Several actions have been fought with enemy escort boats and destroyers, in which we incurred heavy losses; an enemy destroyer was sunk by one of our patrol vessels.

Our escort vessels have been greatly handicapped by small numbers and by weather conditions, and have carried out only minelaying operations. Successful results of our mining operations have been observed. Minesweeping operations have been made off the Scheldt, St. Malo, and the Biscay ports.

Increased fighter-bomber attacks on our small naval craft are being made by day and night. The enemy Air Force is maintaining constant surveillance of all our shipping movements.

III Situation in the air

Fighter, fighter-bomber, and close combat formations are concentrated on the battle area. Every movement made by enemy ground troops (especially in Cherbourg and south-east of Tilly) is strongly supported. Widespread reconnaissance was transformed into active attack almost immediately, and movements

A close-up view of a concrete machine-gun position, which was captured by soldiers of the Regiment de la Chaudières at Bernières-sur-Mer. Having won the first stage of the battle, Canadians are shown gathering behind the sea wall.

were practically impossible. Attacks were directed against troop concentrations, movements of every description, positions, bridges, transport installations, ammunition dumps and recognized Staff Headquarters. Heavy bomber formations operated mainly against special buildings in the V-1 launching sites. Operations were on a smaller scale than last week owing to the weather. Further attacks against airfields and transport installations.

Reconnaissance of rail and road transport was carried out from the battle area as far as the line Paris-Tours-Nantes. Active reconnaissance over the area Nieuport-Velenciennes-Hesdin-Somme estuary, and continual surveillance of the north and west coast of Brittany was maintained.

IV Internal situation

Attitude of the civilian population reserved; in Normandy the friendly attitude towards the Germans noted at first is giving way to definite reserve, and in many places to increased aversion. The number of refugees in the battle area is increasing, among them especially large numbers of able-bodied men. Cases of betrayal of our troop movements are increasing.

Resistance movements and sabotage

The central leadership of a large number of Resistance movements and terrorist groups in the Netherlands is known; little activity so far. Increasing development of Resistance organizations in Belgium and in the frontier area of northern France. Only minor acts of sabotage in Normandy; the Resistance movement has been crippled by the capture of almost all of its leaders.

In spite of successful mopping-up operations and capture of arms and ammunition dumps in Brittany, there has been an increase in sabotage activities towards the end of the week. It is presumed that the enemy's next objective is to bring the terrorist groups, already joined by parachute troops, up to the standard of regular troops by supplying them with weapons and uniforms (in one case 1,000 uniforms were discovered).

V In detail:

Northern Military District:

A. Coastal defenses (Alterations):

(a) Organization of Defense: No changes. 4 draft conducting battalions, provided to safeguard rear positions and defense area, were transferred to 19th Army H.Q. on July 1.

(b) Construction of Atlantic Wall:

Fortifications completed	1,261 emplacements ready for action, 56 more already reinforced with concrete.
Approximate percentage of the whole project completed	69% of the former construction program and plans up to August 30, 1944, completed, 1% reinforced with concrete.
Progress of construction and particular defects	June 23–29, 1944, 8 emplacements ready for action, 9 reinforced with concrete, 23 commenced.
Labour employed	(a) Soldiers: 37,640

(c) Consolidation of the land front: Further consolidation of the land front.

B. Enemy operations on the coast: ./.

C. Operations of enemy aircraft:

(1) Number of raids:

Bombing raids	12 (7)
Strafing raids	16 (21)
Focal point of attacks	0

Total of attacks directed against:

Positions	3 (2)
Building sites	0 (0)
Transport targets	13 (18)
Airfields	4 (4)

(2) Casualties:

Soldiers killed	13 (8)
Soldiers wounded	45 (24)
German civilians killed	2 (0)
German civilians wounded	0 (0)
French civilians killed	18 (24)
French civilians injured	38 (51)

(3) Losses in material:

In attacks on positions	0
In attacks on buildings under construction	0
In attacks on transport targets	5 trucks destroyed, 3 railway cars heavily damaged, 1 River Police boat slightly damaged, 8 locomotives put out of commission, 8 railway passenger carriages and 1 freight railway car burnt out, 2 milk trucks destroyed, 2 trucks damaged.
Unserviceable airfields	0
In attacks on airfields	Minor damage on one airfield.
In other attacks	Blast furnace plant slightly damaged. Damage to civilian property.

(4) Aircraft losses:

Enemy	4
Own	3

D.

(1) Feeling and behavior of the civilian population:
   Unfriendly and expectant.

(2) Instances of sabotage:

Against railways	0
Against cables	0
Against crops	0
Against soldiers	0
Attacks with use of explosives	0
Cases of arson	0

15th Army H.Q.:

A. Coastal defenses (Alterations):

(a) Construction of Atlantic Wall:

Fortifications completed	11 artillery and anti-aircraft positions, 1 tank-gun position, 1 anti-tank pillbox, 5 small emplacements, 1 machine gun site, battle headquarters, anti-tank gun, mortar, machine gun, dummy positions, dugouts for men and ammunition, observation positions, consolidation and mining of beach and air landing obstacles.
Approximate percentage of the whole project completed	49%
Progress of construction and particular defects	According to plan. Lack of cement, wood, material for building positions, tools, and mines of all types. Construc-

After the successful Allied landing June 6, a British MP searches German prisoners of war. As Rommel had predicted, if the invasion were not stopped within the first twenty-four hours, Army Group B would be unable to prevent the Allies from securing a bridgehead.

	tion greatly handicapped by breakdown of electric current.
Labor employed	(a) Soldiers: 20,453 (b) Civilians: 21,279 and 29 prisoners of war. Less than last week in LXXXI Army Corps area.

(b) Consolidation of the land front: Development according to plan. Partially impeded by lack of materials, tools, mines, and labour. Machine gun, anti-tank gun positions, foxholes, dugouts for men and ammunition, observation positions, mortar positions, artillery positions, dugouts for equipment, infantry positions, 4 minefields enclosed, 270 mines laid, 18.5 km. new belt of mines, air landing stakes provided with mines and explosives.

B. Enemy operations on the coast: ./.

C. Operations of enemy aircraft:

(1) Number of raids:

Bombing raids	128 (174)
Strafing raids	28 (31)
Focal point of attacks	Bomber formations: Ostend-Iseghem-Brussels-Florennes-Maubeuge-Valenciennes-Laon-Creil-Montdidier-Doullens-Neufchatel-Etaples. Reconnaissance: Furnes-Tournai-Hesdin-Somme-Etaples-Calais. Fighters and fighter-bombers: Scheldt estuary–Tournai–Dinant–Rethel–Creil–Rouen–Le Havre.

Total of attacks directed against:

Positions	7 (9)
Building sites	26 (79)
Transport targets	88 (75)
Airfields	17 (24)
Other Objectives	18 (18)

(2) Casualties:

Soldiers killed	40 (201)
Soldiers wounded	42 (361)
German civilians killed	1 (1)
French civilians killed	30 (41)
French civilians injured	50 (77)

(3) Losses in material:

In attacks on positions	Destroyed: 1 gun (2 cm.), 1 cookhouse. Damaged: 1 hut, 3 positions,

	minor damage to roads and tracks.
In attacks on buildings under construction	Heavily damaged: 11. Moderately damaged: 2. Slightly damaged: 3.
In attacks on transport targets	Destroyed: 1 electricity plant, 1 transformer station, 19 locomotives, 24 railway cars, railway installations, 1 road, 2 M/T vehicles, 2 dams. Damaged: 12 works buildings, 8 locomotives, 93 railway cars, 1 water tower, 3 cranes, 50 railway installations, 11 M/T vehicles, 2 bridges, telephone and electricity cables.
Unserviceable airfields	Le Culot (Amy, Abbeville-Drucat)
In attacks on airfields	Destroyed: 3 blast bays, 3 hangars, 1 workshop and 2 airfield buildings. Damaged: 6 aircraft, 10 runways, 8 tarmacs, 1 aircraft bay, 6 blast bays, 8 hangars, 1 workshop, 3 airfield buildings, 2 boundary lighting installations, telephone and electricity cables, water mains, 1 narrow gauge railway line.
In other attacks	Destroyed: 1 power station, 1 workshop with 5 M/T vehicles, 1 billet, 1 swingbridge, 2 trucks, 6 cars, 5 motor cycles and a large number of houses, 1 oil tank burnt out. Damaged: 4 industrial plants, 1 power station, 1 M/T repair shop, a large number of houses, electricity and water mains.

(4) Aircraft losses:

Enemy	53 (78)
Own	32 (17)

D.

(1) Feeling and behavior of the civilian population: Unchanged, expectant, reserved, not hostile.

(2) Instances of sabotage:

Against railways	1
Against cables	4
Cases of arson	1

7th Army H.Q.:
Breton Coast:

A. Coastal defenses (Alterations):

(a) Organization of Defense: Defense organization further weakened by withdrawal of 275th Infantry Division.

(b) Construction of Atlantic Wall:

Approximate percentage of the whole project completed	65,882 cubic meters of reinforced concrete of summer construction program used.
Progress of construction and particular defects	910 cubic meters of reinforced concrete during week covered by the report. Construction of field type defenses held up by A-plan and lack of sappers. Concentrated work on coastal defenses and air landing obstacles. Lack of cement and fuel, difficult transport situation and considerable withdrawals of Todt Organization labor is holding up work.

| Labor employed | (a) Soldiers: 20,473 |
| | (b) Civilians: 36,106 |

For the Army Group High Command,

The Chief of General Staff,
Speidel

✠

TO C-IN-C. WEST, JULY 1, 1944

With a view to obtaining unified command of the Wehrmacht and concentration of all forces, I propose to take over command of the headquarters and units of the other two services employed in the Army Group area or cooperating with it.

(1) Luftwaffe

At present there is no question of strategic air warfare. Close cooperation between flying formations and the flak corps and the heavily engaged army can be guaranteed only by the strictest command from <u>one</u> headquarters. Duplication of orders leads to military half measures.

(2) Navy

There is no longer any question of extensive naval strategy. Local tactical operation of the few vessels still at our disposal must be carried out in close cooperation with the movements of the army. The defense of Cherbourg has shown that a unified command and channel of communications are more effective. Finally, the supply situation, especially as regards to transport, demands unified guidance and issue of orders by the Quartermaster General West.

Rommel

CHAPTER 3

The Fall of Caen to the July 20 Assassination Plot, July 3–July 23, 1944

Field Marshal von Kluge arrived at OB West headquarters on July 3, full of confidence and convinced that he would turn the tide of the battle. He proclaimed that Rommel would now learn to take orders and berated his subordinate in front of other officers for his defeatist attitude.[1] It was well known that von Kluge held Hitler's respect and had direct access to the Führer. Stung by von Kluge's harsh criticism, Rommel sent his new C-in-C a lengthy memorandum of the problems encountered by German forces defending Normandy. It was not long, however, before von Kluge began to see these difficulties for himself. Visiting the front, he became aware of Allied air superiority. He witnessed the devastating effects of naval artillery fire in the coastal areas and was shown the destruction wrought by Allied guns with their seemingly unlimited supply of ammunition.

The unpleasant reality of the situation was further reinforced when von Kluge returned to his headquarters at St. Germain to find a new directive from Hitler concerning the conduct of German operations in Normandy.[2] In this memo, the Führer predicted a second Allied landing and ordered the Fifteenth Army to remain in the Pas de Calais. Panzer Group West was to be renamed the Fifth Panzer Army and Eberbach

---

[1] D'Este, 327; Lamb, "Kluge," in Barnett, ed., 405.

[2] Terry Copp and Robert Vogel, *Maple Leaf Route: Falaise, Antwerp & Scheldt* (Alma, ON: Maple Leaf Route, 1987), 41–42.

stepped in to take over from Geyr von Schweppenburg, with orders to pull back from the front and make ready for a counteroffensive. Hitler did not want to hear about the enemy's artillery strength and "inferior" Allied infantry was to be overrun by surprise night attacks conducted without artillery preparation. Normandy was to be held at all costs, and although there were no reinforcements available, every part of France had to be defended against possible further landings. Under Hitler's directive, the well-equipped 11th Panzer Division was scheduled to move from the First Army in southwest France to the Nineteenth Army on the French Mediterranean coast. Three times in July, von Kluge requested that the division be transferred to Normandy, where it was desperately needed, but he was refused on all occasions. Von Kluge's reports on the lack of reinforcements and staggering casualties met the same response as had those of Rommel and von Rundstedt.

The heaviest fighting over the next few days was at Carpiquet, where the 8th Canadian Infantry Brigade attacked the town and airfield on July 4. The fighting around Caen was intensifying, and although the inexperienced 16th Luftwaffe Field Division was brought up to replace the 21st Panzer Division, von Kluge and Rommel decided that the Panzer Lehr would have to be shifted to the American front where the U.S. Army was advancing toward La Haye-du-Puits.

On July 7 the British began their assault on Caen, with 468 heavy bombers dropping 2,562 tons on the city between 9:50 and 10:30 P.M.[3] Operation CHARNWOOD opened with a massive artillery barrage at 4:20 the next morning, using every gun in the Second British Army, as well as offshore naval guns. The 16th Luftwaffe Division's defenses collapsed before the 3rd British Division, while the 59th British and the 3rd Canadian Divisions advanced along a ten-mile front against the 12th SS, driving towards their goal of capturing the city and securing bridgeheads across the Orne River. When the Germans began to withdraw from Caen, the 12th SS mounted a rear-guard

---

[3] Stacey, 158.

action to cover the retreat. The battle at Caen ended on July 9 with heavy casualties on both sides. Major General Kurt Meyer halted the 12th SS withdrawal in the suburbs on the south bank of the Orne, once again preventing Montgomery from achieving his full campaign objectives.

In *bocage* country to the west, the Americans had advanced only five miles in six days and were now encountering fierce opposition as they moved toward Périers. The *bocage*, or hedgerow, country in this area favored the German defenders. Each massive stone hedge, overgrown with trees and thickets, formed a natural defensive position from which German gunners fired unseen at advancing infantry. Tanks and infantry could move only from row to row, and were quickly exposed if they tried to use the narrow roads. As the British and Canadians occupied Caen on July 10, Bradley decided to pause and rest his American formations in order to replace the forty thousand casualties suffered to date.[4] On the Russian front, the Soviet Operation BAGRATION, launched on June 22, was realizing tremendous success against Army Group Center. Germany's line of defense in Russia had been shattered, and the Soviets now launched an offensive against Army Group North, tearing a fifty-mile gap through the German lines in two days of bitter fighting.

By July 11, the Panzer Lehr Division came into action against Bradley's troops in the St. Lô area. Suffering heavy casualties, the Americans were becoming bogged down in the hedgerows of St. Lô and flooded marshlands of Carentan. Bradley called on Montgomery for help, requesting a ten-day respite in order to rebuild and resupply for an American breakout. Monty agreed to launch a British attack to cross the Orne and began planning Operation GOODWOOD, his next effort to break through the German lines outside Caen. A few days later, an ULTRA decrypt confirmed that the Germans were still awaiting a landing by Patton's FUSAG, which they believed would be sent across the Straits of Dover and used to cut off

---

[4] Blumenson, 175.

the German forces in Normandy. Churchill sent the decrypt to Roosevelt on July 15 with a notation that "Uncertainty is a terror to the Germans."[5]

The continuing success of FORTITUDE, now five weeks after the D-Day landings, is also confirmed in a memo written by Rommel on July 15. He wrote to von Kluge that Army Group B had lost ninety-seven thousand men since June 6 but had received only six thousand replacements. Seventeen tanks had been sent to replace the 225 lost. Overwhelming Allied air and artillery superiority was smashing the German army in Normandy to pieces. He further noted that no new forces could be brought up to the Normandy front except by weakening the Fifteenth Army on the Channel or the Mediterranean forces stationed in southern France. Rommel asked von Kluge to forward the report directly to Hitler. The next day, Rommel also sought Hitler's permission to withdraw the twenty-eight thousand German troops stationed in the Channel Islands. Hitler refused.[6]

On July 17 Rommel set out for his daily tour of the front. After visiting the 276th and 277th Infantry Divisions, he continued on to Sepp Dietrich's Headquarters, where he met with Dietrich and Meyer. Expecting a British attack within twenty-four hours, Rommel wanted Meyer's 12th SS to support the 272nd Infantry Division. His daily tour completed, Rommel left in his staff car, but on his way back to La Roche–Guyon, he was spotted and attacked by two Spitfires. In the ensuing car crash, Rommel suffered severe head injuries. Unconscious and covered with blood, he was taken first to a shelter and then to the hospital at St. Germain. He would never return to the battlefield. Von Kluge was placed at the head of Army Group B in addition to his posting as C-in-C West.[7] He moved from OB West headquarters at St. Germain to those of Army Group B at La Roche–Guyon.

As Rommel had predicted, the Allies renewed their offensive the next day. Montgomery's Operation GOODWOOD, the

---

[5] Hinsley, 216.
[6] Gilbert, 556.
[7] OKW, 55.

largest offensive yet launched against German lines, was sent across the Orne on July 18, led by the British VIII Corps with the Canadian II Corps supporting the right flank. Across the river, the 1st SS Panzer *Leibstandarte* Division was dug in at Bourguébus Ridge southeast of Caen. To the west, Bradley's American forces entered St. Lô that same day. Both attacks soon broke down into heavy fighting, with the British attack being brought to a halt by elements of the 21st Panzer Division. Eberbach had anticipated Montgomery's offensive and deployed the forces of the I SS Panzer and LXXXVI Corps in four defensive belts nearly ten miles deep, with a fifth belt acting as a reserve.[8]

Heavy losses in both men and tanks were sustained on both sides. For two days of bitter fighting, Canadian and British forces fought their way to the third belt of defense, but the German gun line on the crest of Bourguébus Ridge remained intact. On the afternoon of July 20, just as Montgomery's troops were preparing to assault the ridge, a prolonged downpour turned the battlefield into a sea of mud, ending the siege with gains and losses for both sides. The battle had exhausted the German panzer divisions and prevented their transfer to the American sector south of the Cotentin. To meet the British and Canadian assault at Caen, two panzer divisions that had been moving to the American front were recalled. The Germans, however, still held vital ground at Verrières Ridge. Rommel's defensive zone held firm but constant air attacks dropping twelve thousand tons of bombs were taking their toll. The demoralization of senior German commanders at this time is reflected in the Army Group B situation reports: "The extraordinary vigour and the colossal material superiority of the enemy in the fighting east of Caen on July 18 and 19 are indicated by the fact that he fired 103,000 artillery shells on the left flank of the 86th Corps and the 1st SS Panzer alone, and according to his own reports, dropped in our positions 7,800 tons of bombs from 2,200 two and four-engined bombers."

---

[8] D'Este, 377.

The bad weather of July 20 also affected the battle in the *bocage*. The Americans had to postpone their proposed breakout from St. Lô, code-named Operation COBRA, until the twenty-fifth. American and German casualties were extremely high in this sector, particularly for the German 352nd Division, which was still holding the line after its stubborn defense of Omaha Beach. This division almost ceased to exist after St. Lô, where its casualties contributed to the total of 116,000 suffered by the Seventh Army since June 6. To replace these losses, only ten thousand reinforcements were received, drawn from the *Ersatzheer* (Replacement Army) in Germany. Of the nearly six hundred tanks destroyed, only seventeen replacements had arrived. The strength of the perimeter drawn around the Allied lodgment in Normandy was stretched close to the breaking point.

As the weather brought a halt to the fighting around Caen and St. Lô, a group of German army officers made an attempt to assassinate Hitler in his Wolf's Lair headquarters in Rastenburg. On July 20, Colonel von Stauffenberg placed a bomb under the conference table where Hitler, Keitel, Jodl, Warlimont, and eighteen others studied the war plans before them. He then left the room on the excuse of having to take a phone call and was outside the building when the bomb exploded. Believing Hitler to be dead, von Stauffenberg was on his way to Berlin to join General Beck and other highly placed army conspirators in establishing a new government. Convinced that Hitler was destroying the fatherland and an entire generation of its young men in his obsession to fight an unwinnable two-front war, their goal was to negotiate a separate peace with the British and Americans. Unknown to von Stauffenberg, in his absence the briefcase containing the bomb had been pushed farther back against the supports of the heavy oak table, which then shielded Hitler from the blast.[9] The Führer emerged with one hundred splinters from the map table in his legs, but he was alive.

---

[9] D'Este, 399.

In Berlin there was much confusion, as it was initially unclear whether or not Hitler had survived the assassination attempt. Most of his field commanders stayed loyal not so much from their personal oath but more from the fact that Germany was still fighting and their knowledge that the Allies had committed themselves to an unconditional surrender. At Army Group B headquarters, von Kluge delayed. Word came from Berlin that Hitler had survived an assassination plot, along with additional instructions that any orders from Generals Fromm and Hoepner and Field Marshal Witzleben were to be disregarded. Von Kluge was aware of the plot,[10] but he delayed before accepting the conspirators' orders, which were sent out from Berlin in the mistaken assumption that Hitler had been killed.[11] He called Beck in Berlin, then Rastenburg, and finally von Stauffenberg, who again assured von Kluge that the Führer was indeed dead. For two hours von Kluge discussed the momentous developments with Blumentritt, his chief of staff. The military governor of France, von Stülpnagel, arrived at La Roche–Guyon to ask for von Kluge's endorsement of the plot. Then he received a call from OB West headquarters at St. Germain confirming Keitel's message that Hitler was alive and that orders were to be taken from no one but himself or the SS chief, Himmler. To Blumentritt, von Kluge confessed, "Today I am without hope." A little later, he dictated a congratulatory message to the Führer, condemning the murderous attempt against his life and assuring him of "our unalterable loyalty."

The next morning, von Kluge wrote a letter to Hitler to demonstrate his innocence and distance himself from the conspirators. He attached Rommel's letter written on July 15, two days prior to his accident. Von Kluge had earlier hesitated to forward this letter due to its outspoken criticisms, but in light of the July 20 plot, he probably did not want to be found holding onto "defeatist" correspondence from a possible conspirator who believed that "the unequal struggle is nearing its end."

---

[10] Blumenson, 147.
[11] Müller, "Witzleben, Stülpnagel, and Speidel," in Barnett, ed., 63.

Yet by July 22 it appears that the realities of the Normandy situation once again became foremost in von Kluge's thoughts, as he called Jodl to say that the whole Normandy front was a disastrous mess and ask whether Hitler fully appreciated the tremendous consumption of German forces over the last few weeks. He continued that his infantry could not last much longer, that there were too few troops with which to hold the line. A few hours later, he received Hitler's response: "Stand fast."

The Führer later wired his commanders: "Anyone who gives up an inch of ground will be shot." Addressing the Normandy commanders specifically, he added, "Anyone who speaks of peace without victory will lose his head, no matter who he is or what his position." Through the Gestapo, Hitler already knew of the connection between Rommel, von Kluge, and the conspiracy. Far from weakening the Führer's position, the assassination attempt had actually left him more powerful than ever as it provided the opportunity to maintain closer watch over his generals. Any freedom to question his judgment was now gone, as criticism would indicate a connection to the conspiracy. The Waffen-SS was raised to equal status with the Wehrmacht, Luftwaffe, and Kriegsmarine.

More than 150 conspirators were executed or committed suicide in the aftermath of the of the July 20 plot. Those who survived now found themselves fighting against increasingly difficult odds. In the first days of August, Hitler ordered an all-out counterattack near Mortain, both as a test of the German army's loyalty and as a bid to produce a strategic reversal of the military situation in the west. Hitler's Operation LÜTTICH would use all available armor to drive into the flank of the American spearhead emerging south from St. Lô, smashing through the interior of Brittany and the *bocage* country and on towards the sea.

✠

WEEKLY REPORT, JULY 3–9, 1944

I Estimate of the situation as a whole.

During the period covered by the report, the 2nd British Army and the 1st American Army, using unusually large masses of men and material in a large-scale attack, attempted to break through in order to conduct operations in open country.

The prelude was a local attack on July 3 concentrated on a 7 km. front in the area in front of Caen, which resulted in the loss of Carpiquet after heavy fighting. On July 8 the enemy launched a concentrated attack on Caen with at least three infantry divisions, several armored brigades, and strong H.Q. troops, after having bombarded the whole area during the previous night with naval land and artillery of all calibers (80,000 rounds) and with continual air attacks (approximately 2,500 tons). After two days of very heavy fighting the enemy, who suffered particularly heavy losses of men and material (the 12th SS Panzer Division alone knocked out 103 tanks) succeeded in smashing the bridgehead and taking Caen. The enemy was not successful in effecting a breakthrough, however, as a secure defense had been built up in time on the Orne.

On July 10 the attacks were continued, concentrated on both sides of Verson, and are still in progress.

Fighting on the rest of the Panzer Group West front was only in the nature of local holding operations.

On the 7th Army front with 4–5 infantry divisions and strong armored forces, the enemy launched a north-south thrust on July 3 between Prairies Marécageuses de Gorges and the west coast. In spite of ruthless employment of men, massed artillery, and air forces, the enemy was prevented from breaking through. An area of approximately 5 km. in depth had to be relinquished to the enemy in the course of the week; fighting continues on the line Plessis-Mobecq-Bretteville.

From July 4 the enemy extended his attacks to the Vire. After having succeeded in establishing bridgeheads over the Vire and Taute, he attempted to break through into the area

In early June, Colonel Kurt Meyer (left), commander of the 25th
Panzer Grenadier Regiment, talks with other 12th SS officers,
Brigadier General Fritz Witt (center) and Lieutenant Colonel Max
Wünsche, in the courtyard of the Abbaye d'Ardennes. The 12th SS
"Hitler Youth" Division came into action on June 7 and consisted of
sixteen- to eighteen-year-old men who had been specially selected
for their determination and devotion to Hitler.

St. Lo–Periers–Coutances. In heavy battles he was prevented
from making a decisive breakthrough. The 2nd SS Panzer Division and the Panzer Training Division were brought up to the
battle area, and some units took part in the fighting. The 5th
Paratroop Division is being brought up.

The enemy has once more failed to reach his breakthrough objectives this week, and has suffered heavy casualties.
The 101st and 82nd American Airborne Divisions have already
been withdrawn owing to heavy losses, but have been replaced
by fresh divisions.

From June 6 to July 9 the enemy lost 1,297 armored vehicles and 266 aircraft through the action of army and SS units.

Even when compared with the heavy enemy losses, our losses are also considerable. From June 6 to July 7 they amount to:—

1,830	officers (including 9 generals, 7 officers of the General Staff, and 109 C.O.'s)
75,166	NCO's and men
3,787	Russians
80,783	

Enemy strength and operational plans.

It is estimated that the enemy has at present 35 divisions and strong H.Q. troops in the landing area. In Great Britain a further 60 large formations are standing by, of which 50 could be transferred to the Continent at any time.

According to indications, and data, the plans of the Montgomery Army Group are just as we expect. After taking the whole of the Caen area and throwing adequate bridgeheads over the Orne the enemy intends to commence the thrust on Paris, in the course of which a large-scale landing must be expected in the 15th Army Zone by the 1st American Army Group to cooperate with the Montgomery Army Group and to eliminate the long range weapon.

According to a captured order, the American 1st Army's primary objective is the extension and consolidation of their land base by the occupation of the St. Lo–Coutances area and later the line Vire-Avranches. The strategy of attrition of both armies can be recognized by the use of masses of material and ammunition.

To improve our freedom of action, while at the same time preventing a breakthrough, Army Group B will attempt to withdraw panzer formations and replace them by infantry divisions.

Owing to lack of transport space and the delaying effect of air attacks, the supply position is very critical as regards ammunition and fuel, in spite of some slight improvement in transport up to the front.

II Situation at sea:

More intensive surveillance of the sea area off Le Havre and Cap d'Antifer by strong groups of enemy destroyers and escort vessels. Numerous naval actions.

Increasing control of the Channel Island area and the northern coast of Brittany by enemy destroyers and other naval forces.

Widespread use of battleships, cruisers and destroyers in bombardment of the coast and in support of the enemy attack on Caen.

Considerable enemy supply and reinforcement traffic; a temporary decrease was noticeable after our small naval craft had been sent into action.

Numerous fighter-bomber attacks on our defense forces. Air surveillance of the whole Channel coast, including coastal and outer routes between Brest and La Pallice. 3 fighter-bomber attacks on naval radar stations in the area of Cap d'Antifer and on Ile d'Oussant.

Enemy mining activity slight in comparison with last week.

III Situation in the air

Very heavy enemy air activity, only temporarily held up by weather conditions.

Fighter and fighter-bomber sorties were concentrated in the battle area in support of ground troops. Continual attacks against positions of every description, ammunition and supply dumps, and against movements far to the rear. Isolated fighter-bomber sorties as far as the Loire. Strong fighter forces covering the battle area and making operations by the Luftwaffe difficult.

Twin-engined formations directed attacks against transport installations (stations, trains, bridges, ferries and crossroads) and against troop concentrations.

Heavy bomber formations strongly supported by fighters attacked construction sites and special installations in the V-1 launching sites, marshalling yards and airfields.

Reconnaissance was made of rail, road and water transport as far as the line Rheims-Orleans-Angers-Rennes. Constant surveillance was noticeable in the Ostend–Lens–Amiens–Le Tréport area and of the north and west coast of Brittany.

IV Internal situation;

Attitude of the civilian population still reserved and expectant.

Resistance organizations and sabotage:

It has been confirmed that British and French parachute groups have been landed in areas outside Brittany to reinforce and direct the Resistance movement. Still relatively slight activity in the Netherlands. In Belgium and the frontier area of northern France: a marked increase of partisan activity. The British radio is sending an increased number of code words to Resistance groups.

The number of attacks and acts of sabotage, which has been exceptionally high since the end of June, has risen still further in the last few days. Heavy sabotage of electric cables during the night of July 6–7.

Normandy: partisan activity has spread to areas formerly free of terrorists (Pont Audemer), and also in the battle area (Caen). Roads in rear areas have been covered with small mines.

Brittany: increasing sabotage of railway installations and long distance electricity cables. Attacks on small detachments of troops and freight trains reveal planned preparation and military direction (concentrated in the area Guingamp-Lannion); however no large-scale military use of partisan bands has been made. Concentration area of terrorist supply in southern Brittany, with up to 40 machines in one night.

In detail:

Northern Military District:

A. *Coastal defenses (Alterations):*

(a) Organization of Defense: No changes.

(b) Construction of Atlantic Wall:

Fortifications completed	1,270 positions ready for action, 54 others reinforced with concrete.
Approximate percentage of the whole project completed	70% completed, 1% reinforced with concrete, of construction programme and planning up to August 30.
Progress of construction and particular defects	June 30–July 6: 9 positions ready for action, 7 reinforced with concrete, 5 positions newly begun.
Labor employed	About 15,470 in fortress type and about 36,000 in field type construction.

(c) Consolidation of the land front: Further consolidation of the land front.

B. *Enemy operations on the coast: ./.*

C. *Operations of enemy aircraft:*

(1) Number of raids:

Bombing raids	0 (0)
Strafing raids	0 (0)
Focal point of attacks	0 (0)

Total of attacks directed against:

Positions	0 (3)
Building sites	0 (0)
Transport targets	9 (13
Airfields	5 (4)

(2) Casualties:

Soldiers killed	8 (13)
Soldiers wounded	8 (45)
German civilians killed	0 (2)
German civilians wounded	0 (0)
French civilians killed	26 (18)
French civilians injured	42 (38)

(3) Losses in material:

In attacks on positions	0
In attacks on buildings under construction	0
In attacks on transport targets	One railway and one road bridge damaged, 7 locomotives put out of commission, 10 freight railway cars containing army trucks destroyed by fire, 11 freight railway cars slightly damaged.
Unserviceable airfields	0
In attacks on airfields	Runways, tarmacs and buildings damaged, 6 Ju 88s damaged.
In other attacks	Numerous houses destroyed and damaged.

(4) Aircraft losses:

Enemy	9
Own	1

An observation post at the Abbaye d'Ardennes. Meyer established his headquarters here after the 12th SS made a slow advance to the front, its vehicles and 20,000 men impeded by Allied air attacks and blocked roads.

D.

(1) Feeling and behavior of the civilian population: Unchanged.

(2) Instances of sabotage:

Against railways	0
Against cables	0
Against crops	0
Against soldiers	1
Attacks with use of explosives	0
Cases of arson	0

15th Army H.Q.:

A. Coastal defenses (Alterations):

(a) Organization of Defense: Defense organization in Le Havre area reinforced after arrival of 89th Division.

(b) Construction of Atlantic Wall:

Fortifications completed	1 artillery pillbox, 6 pillboxes, 2 small dugouts, machine gun, anti-tank gun, anti-aircraft, tank gun, mortar, dummy positions (fortress type), ammunition and Goliath dugouts, Tobruk positions, consolidation and mining of beach and air landing obstacles. Main area of consolidation at river estuaries. Work started on installation of beacons on immediate front.
Approximate percentage of the whole project completed	64%
Progress of construction and particular defects	In general, according to plan. Held up by lack of cement, material for building positions and mines, also partly by interruptions caused by air raids. Employment of Todt Organization labour greatly restricted in parts.
Labor employed	(a) Soldiers: 22,618 (b) Civilians: 22,828 and 29 prisoners of war.

(c) Consolidation of the land front: Foxholes, machine gun,
anti-tank gun, mortar, anti-aircraft positions, dugouts for
men, ammunition, equipment, horses and supplies, observation posts, artillery positions, battle headquarters, shelters, splinter bays for vehicles, fencing in of minefields,
478 anti-personnel and 660 anti-tank mines laid, work
started on the Boulogne land front, air landing stakes provided with mines and shells at Le Havre; 1,600 anti-tank
and 1,900 anti-personnel mines laid. Construction greatly
handicapped by lack of labour, mining and construction
material (especially wood and wire) as well as lack of
trenching and other tools.

B. Enemy operations on the coast: ./.

C. Operations of enemy aircraft:

(1) Number of raids:

Bombing raids	118 (128)
Strafing raids	31 (28)
Focal point of attacks	Bomber formations: Brussels, Cambrai, Amiens, Beauvais, Dieppe, Somme estuary, Boulogne, Armentieres, Chauny, Rethel, Abbeville. Reconnaissance: Ostend, Lens, Amiens, Le Treport. Fighters and fighter-bombers: Scheldt estuary, Courtrai, Maubeuge, Laon, Montdidier, St. Valery e. C.

Total of attacks directed against:

Positions	12 (7)
Building sites	59 (26)
Transport targets	59 (88)
Airfields	9 (17)
Other targets	10 (18)

(2) Casualties:

Soldiers killed	48 (40)
Soldiers wounded	20 (42)
German civilians killed	— (1)
French civilians killed	67 (30)
French civilians injured	22 (50)

(3) Losses in material:

In attacks on positions	Destroyed: 3 huts, 5 ammunition bunkers, 1 anti-aircraft gun (10.5 cm.), 2 M/T vehicles, 1 ammunition depot. Damaged: 3 ammunition bunkers, 1 railway installation, 1 building, 2 trucks, several huts, roads and cables, 2 light anti-aircraft trains buried, 100 rounds of anti-aircraft ammunition blown up.
In attacks on buildings under construction	Heavily damaged: 11, Medium damage: 3, Slightly damaged: 7.
In attacks on transport targets	Destroyed: 1 works building, 2 works installations, 1 railway bridge, 31 locomotives, 52 railway cars, 1 road, 1 dam, several railway installations, 2 vessels sunk. Damaged: 8 works buildings, 4 locomotives, 84 railway cars, several roads, a large number of railway installations, 6 vessels.
Unserviceable airfields	(Arques, Chambry, Coxyde, Diest, Juvincourt, Liegescourt, Poix-Ost, St. Pol–Brias, Ursel, Vlamerthinghe, Wizernes)

In attacks on airfields	Destroyed: 1 ammunition dump. Damaged: 2 runways, 1 tarmac, 4 blast bays and several buildings.
In other attacks	Destroyed: 1 road, a large number of houses. Damaged: 3 gasometers, a large number of houses.

(4) Aircraft losses:

Enemy	From June 25–July 1: 57 (53)
Own	31 (32)

D.

(1) Feeling and behavior of the civilian population: Unchanged, reserved and expectant.

(2) Instances of sabotage:

Against railways	One attempt.
Against cables	3
Against soldiers	2

7th Army H.Q.:

A. Coastal defenses (Alterations):

(a) Organization of Defense: Further weakening of defenses in Brittany after withdrawal of the 5th Paratroop Division and the 275th Infantry Division from their former coastal defense sectors.

(b) Construction of Atlantic Wall:

Fortifications completed	Nil return.
Approximate percentage of the whole project completed	66,800 cubic meters of reinforced concrete.

Field Marshal Gerd von Rundstedt, Major Hubert Meyer (staff officer of the 12th SS), Lieutenant General Sepp Dietrich (commander of the I SS Panzer Corps), Brigadier General Fritz Witt of the 12th SS, and Colonel Kurt Meyer of the 25th Panzer Grenadiers are shown, right to left. General Witt was killed on June 12 and replaced by Kurt Meyer, who at age thirty-three became the youngest divisional commander in the German forces. Dietrich later took command of the Fifth Panzer Army during the escape from the Falaise Pocket and, later, the Sixth Panzer Army during the German "Miracle in the West" in the autumn of 1944.

Progress of construction and particular defects	515 cubic meters construction of field type positions further impeded. Increased difficulties in completing fortress and field type constructions. Terrorist menace is making employment of civilians more difficult.
Labor employed	Coastal front: (a) Soldiers: 2,500 (b) Civilians: 3,200

Land front:
(a) Soldiers: 3,700
(b) Civilians: 10,200

For the Army Group High Command,

The Chief of General Staff,
Speidel

WEEKLY REPORT, JULY 10–16, 1944

I Estimate of the situation as a whole.

The 2nd British Army has not achieved its aim of breaking through and operating in open country after the capture of Caen, when further attacks broke down owing to heavy losses. A counter-attack by our troops on July 11 was successful, and the former main defense line south of the Odon (south-west of Caen) was retaken; after this the enemy remained quiet, except for local infantry and considerable artillery activity. Regrouping and preparations on an increasing scale were observed towards the end of the week. In the early hours of July 16 the enemy commenced local attacks between Maltot and Vendes, and these are still in progress. An offensive by the 2nd British Army to break towards the south-east can be expected from the evening of July 17.

On the 7th Army sector the enemy attempted to break through and force the capture of St. Lo area in battles which are intensifying daily. Once more the enemy failed to reach his objective, but sectors 3 km. to 5 km. in depth to the north-east and north-west of St. Lo had to be yielded to him. After a defensive success on the northern front LXXXIV Army Corps fell back without enemy interference to the Seves-Lessay sector during the night of July 13/14. The enemy has not yet completely closed up on the main defense line.

Enemy attacks concentrated on the St. Lo area are continuing on the same scale.

During the period between June 6 and July 16, the enemy suffered the following losses through the actions of the army and SS units

1,705 tanks and 293 aircraft

Our own losses from June 6 to July 7 amount to:

2,360	officers (including 9 generals, 7 officers of the General Staff, 137 C.O.'s.)
93,938	NCO's and men
3,791	Russians

100,089 men

Replacements since June 6:

8,395 men brought up to the front

5,303 men warned for transfer to the front.

The replacement situation gives rise to some anxiety in view of increasing losses. Some remedy must be found before units are depleted.

Enemy strength and operational plans:

Enemy supply of men and material continues without interruption, and it is estimated that there are approximately 37 divisions and strong H.Q. troops in the landing area. According to the distribution of enemy forces the following minimum artillery strengths are estimated, exclusive of naval artillery:

2nd British Army:
      270 light batteries   50 medium and heavy batteries

1st American Army:
      130 light batteries   135 medium and heavy batteries

Total of at least:
      400 light batteries   185 medium and heavy batteries

In Great Britain a further 56 large formations are at ready, of which 46 can be transferred to the Continent.

One of the Panzer Lehr Division Panther tanks destroyed at Bret-
teville-l'Orgueilleuse during heavy fighting on the night of June 8/9.
It was taken out by fire from a PIAT (projector infantry anti-tank) in
a hard-fought, but ultimately unsuccessful effort to drive the Allied
forces back into the sea.

The known operational plans of the Montgomery Army
Group still appear to remain the same.

The 2nd British Army is clearly concentrated in the area of
Caen and to the south-west, and plans to make a thrust across
the Orne towards Paris. The local attacks between Maltot and
Vendes, which commenced on July 15 may be regarded as the
preliminary to the offensive to break through over the Orne
expected from July 17.

The 1st American Army will continue its plan to extend its
land base up to the line Domfront-Avranches, using heavy concentrations of men and materials.

1st American Army Group: There are no fresh indications
of the objectives of the 1st American Army Group. A large-scale
landing must be expected in the area of the 15th Army, for
strategic cooperation with Montgomery's Army Group, where
the main weight of the enemy operations appears to be con-

centrated, and for the elimination of long distance weapons. Agents' reports of an intended landing in southern Brittany contradict the distribution of forces reported in Great Britain.

Army Group B will continue its attempt to prevent all efforts to break through. The replacement of panzer formations by infantry units has not yet produced the desired result. Compared with the modern Anglo-American units, the infantry divisions are so inferior in equipment and strength that most of the reserve panzer groups had to be sent into action again.

II Situation at sea:

Close patrol of the sea area off the landing area and Cap d'Antifer–Le Havre by enemy destroyer and MTB groups.

Numerous naval actions. According to a reliable source a number of enemy vessels have struck mines.

Extended and reinforced enemy patrols (including heavy cruisers) off the coast of Brittany as far as Lorient, concentrated on Brest. Surprise appearance of enemy destroyer group off the Ile de Croix.

Fighter-bomber attacks were carried out against our defense forces along the whole Channel coast and also on the Atlantic coast as far as St. Nazaire.

Extensive supply movements by transports, freighters and LSTs in the landing area. Supply by small craft is decreasing.

Air reconnaissance of Cherbourg found only landing craft and low-tonnage steamers in the outer harbor, which must be presumed cleared. Large-scale unloading unlikely. Large-scale unloading activity in the landing area confirms the view that 17 days after the fall of Cherbourg there is no possibility of unloading in the inner harbour.

Enemy mining activity in the Channel has diminished, and is slight on the Atlantic coast.

III Situation in the air:

In spite of being hindered by bad weather conditions, strong fighter and fighter-bomber forces were almost continually active over the battle and rear areas. Considerably fewer sorties were made by heavy bomber formations owing to heavy attacks on Germany. Heavy bomber formations directed their attacks mainly against V-1 launching sites, transport installations and airfields. Most of the attacks by twin-engined bomber formations were directed against railway installations.

By day and night fighter and fighter-bomber formations attacked supply routes and positions of every description in the main defense zone as well as covering the battle area. Repeated attacks were made on bridges, ferries and railway targets as far as the line Paris-Tours-Vannes.

Reconnaissance aircraft maintained constant surveillance of rail, road and water transport as far as the line Chalons s.M.–Orleans–Angers and the coastal area of Brittany.

IV Internal situation:

The attitude of the civilian population continues expectant, and to some extent unfriendly. In the Belgian coastal area some of the population volunteered for work on defenses following measures to evacuate the coastal combat area.

Resistance organizations and sabotage:

Slight increase in sabotage activity; progressive development of Resistance organizations, but no large-scale operations as yet.

Attacks on economic and municipal officials, Dutch police and National Socialist Party members.

Belgium and Northern France: sporadic sabotage of cables during the night of July 11/12, otherwise no increase in sabotage. Indications of progressive mobilization of Resistance movements in the interior.

Normandy: increased laying of small mines on roads. Isolated arson attempts on vehicles.

Brittany: no numerical increase in acts of sabotage. Attacks are well planned however and reveal leadership by trained men. The supply system has been hardest hit by numerous explosions on railway tracks, and by attacks with explosives on locomotive depots and ammunition trains.

Destruction of railway bridges, especially in northern Brittany. Several attacks on power supply. Numerous attacks on members of the Wehrmacht. Areas of concentration: Lannion-Plouarot and Pontivy-Loudeac-Carhaix.

The further development of Resistance organizations has not been appreciably hindered by our intervention, and planned development of fighting groups must be expected. Main area where terrorist bands are being formed is to the south of Pontivy. Enemy losses: 168 dead (including 16 parachutists), 117 prisoners (including 4 parachutists).

Northern Military District:

A. Coastal defenses (Alterations):

(a) Organization of Defense: The battle group of the 19th Panzer Division transferred at 1800 hours on July 15. The remaining units of the division are in the former billeting area with orders to defend it against landings from the air.

(b) Construction of Atlantic Wall:

Fortifications completed	1,288 positions
Approximate percentage of the whole project completed	71% of program up to September 30, 1944, completed.
Progress of construction and particular defects	18 positions ready for action, 7 reinforced with concrete.
Labor employed	No important changes.

(c) Consolidation of the land front: Further consolidation of the land front.

B. Enemy operations on the coast:
None.

C. Operations of enemy aircraft:

(1) Number of raids:

Bombing raids	5 (7)
Strafing raids	2 (9)
Focal point of attacks	0 (0)

Total of attacks directed against:

Positions	0 (0)
Building sites	0 (0)
Transport targets	2 (9)
Airfields	0 (5)

(2) Casualties:

Soldiers killed	0 (8)
Soldiers wounded	2 (8)
German civilians killed	0 (0)
German civilians wounded	0 (0)
French civilians killed	0 (26)
French civilians injured	1 (42)

(3) Losses in material:

In attacks on positions	0
In attacks on buildings under construction	0
In attacks on transport targets	1 barge and 1 vehicle damaged.
Unserviceable airfields	0
In attacks on airfields	0
In other attacks	Slight damage to houses.

(4) Aircraft losses:

Enemy	4
Own	7

On July 1, 1944, von Rundstedt asked permission from OKW to begin a planned withdrawal to a more defensible line south of Caen, but his request was denied by Hitler. Convinced that von Rundstedt had lost faith in ultimate victory, Hitler replaced him with Field Marshal Günther von Kluge, although Rundstedt was later appoitned C-in-C West and oversaw the German recovery in the West and the Ardennes counteroffensive. U.S. HOLOCAUST MEMORIAL MUSEUM

D.

(1) Feeling and behavior of the civilian population: Unchanged, expectant and unfriendly.

(2) Instances of sabotage:

Against railways	0
Against cables	0
Against crops	0
Against soldiers	0
Attacks with use of explosives	0
Cases of arson	1

15th Army H.Q.:

A. Coastal defenses (Alterations):

(a) Organization of Defense: Army defense organization weakened after withdrawal of 326th and 363rd Infantry Divisions.

(a) Construction of Atlantic Wall:

Fortifications completed	2 gun and 1 anti-aircraft pillbox positions, 1 tank gun, 1 anti-tank gun 8.8 cm., and 1 7.5 cm. anti-tank gun position, 2 other pillbox positions (field type), machine gun, mortar, anti-tank gun and artillery positions, bunkers, reserve and dummy positions, consolidation and reinforcement of beach and airlanding obstacles by installation of explosives and anti-personnel mines, 1 60-ton bridge constructed and 1 minefield laid.
Approximate percentage of the whole project completed	Approximately 66%.
Progress of construction and particular defects	Lack of building material (especially cement and sawn wood), labour, transport and mines. Progress hampered measures taken under Alarm II.
Labor employed	(a) Soldiers: 22,136 (b) Civilians: 21,988 and 32 POWs.

(c) Consolidation of the land front: Machine gun, mortar, anti-tank, and artillery positions, bunkers, foxholes, observation positions, battle positions; new mining: Boulogne fortress (commenced), and Le Havre land front, and a further 10.5 km. 924 anti-tank and 90 anti-personnel mines laid.

B. Enemy operations on the coast: ./.

C. Operations of enemy aircraft:

(1) Number of raids:

Bombing raids	53 (118)
Strafing raids	16 (31)
Focal point of attacks	Bomber formations: St. Omer, Arras, Albert, Montdidier, Chateau Thierry, Beauvais, Gisors, Aumale, Dieppe, Amiens, Abbeville. Reconnaissance: Scheldt estuary, Brussels, Charleroi, Valenciennes, Calais. Fighters and fighter-bombers: Scheldt estuary, Brussels, Charleville, St. Quentin, Soissons, St. Valery en Caux.

Total of attacks directed against:

Positions	6 (12)
Building sites	23 (59)
Transport targets	24 (59)
Airfields	12 (9)
Other targets	4 (10)

(2) Casualties:

Soldiers killed	21 (without aircraft crews) (48)
Soldiers wounded	20 (without aircraft crews) (29)

German civilians killed	10 (—)
German civilians wounded	1 (—)
French civilians killed	13 (67)
French civilians injured	10 (22)

(3) Losses in material:

In attacks on positions	Destroyed: 2 four-barrelled guns, 1 searchlight. Damaged: 1 special trailer 202, railway installations, damage to windows. 1 anti-aircraft and battery control position buried.
In attacks on buildings under construction	Destroyed: 1. Heavy damage: 7. Medium damage: 4. Slight damage: 6.
In attacks on transport targets	Destroyed: 1 railway bridge, 5 locomotives, 2 motor vehicles, 14 railway cars (including 8 with ammunition), various approach roads. Damaged: 2 railway works buildings, 1 transformer station, 1 railway bridge, 1 road bridge, 3 reservoirs, 4 locomotives, 19 railway cars, 2 huts, tracks, telephone communications, 1 dam. 2 vessels sunk.
Unserviceable airfields	Mons en Chaussee, Poix-Nord
In attacks on airfields	Destroyed: 2 empty fuelling installations, 1 hangar, 2 airfield buildings. Damaged: 2 runways, 3 tarmacs, 1 set boundary lighting and telephone cables.

A reinforced concrete bunker at Carpiquet shown after its capture by Allied forces in July 1944. In a fierce three-day battle for the airfield, Canadian infantry, British armor, RAF typhoons, and fire from the battleship HMS *Rodney* were matched by German counterattacks with several 88s and more than twenty dug-in tanks.

In other attacks	Destroyed: a large number of houses (exact figures not known), 2 trucks (1 with load of cable). Damaged: 1 bridge, 1 road, a large number of houses, telephone lines and water mains, damage to cultivated fields.

(4) Aircraft losses:

Enemy	49 (57)

D.

(1) Feeling and behavior of the civilian population:
    Unchanged, reserved and expectant.

(2) Instances of sabotage:

CAgainst railways	1
Against cables	25
Against soldiers	1
Attacks with use of explosives	2

Panzer Group West:

Further consolidation of the land front in 711th Infantry Division sector. Considerable lack of building materials and transport difficulties are holding up work. For other details, see report on situation as a whole.

7th Army H.Q.:

A. Coastal defenses (Alterations):

(a) Organization of Defense: Brittany: Defense considerably
    weakened by withdrawal of 5th Paratroop Division and
    275th Infantry Division.

(b) Construction of Atlantic Wall:

Approximate percentage of the whole project completed	From summer construction program: 67,098 cubic meters of reinforced concrete.
Progress of construction and particular defects	698 cubic meters of reinforced concrete. Difficulties described in the report for the last week have further increased. Shortages of engineers and supervisors.

Labor employed	On the coastal front:
	(a) Soldiers: 8,533
	(b) Civilians: 6,323.
	On the land front:
	(a) Soldiers: 1,550
	(b) Civilians: 3,521.

For the Army Group High Command,

The Chief of General Staff,
Speidel

WEEKLY REPORT, JULY 17–23, 1944

I Estimate of the situation as a whole:

On July 17, the 2nd British and the 1st American Armies began their large-scale attack from the Caen and St. Lo areas in an attempt to force a strategic breakthrough. In spite of their powerful air support and their superior artillery, this plan failed.

On July 18, after a heavy preliminary bombardment from land and sea artillery, and intensive bombing from over 1,000 aircraft, the attack in the area of Panzer Group West was begun from the bridgehead east of the Orne, launched with 4 infantry divisions, 3 armored divisions and 2 to 3 armored brigades. As a result of the intensive bombardment the enemy succeeded in breaking through across the line Touffreville–Colombelles to the south. With our last reserves we engaged the enemy in bitter fighting along the line west of Troarn–south of Frenouville–St. Andre–Bougie. The weather caused a slackening off in the fighting towards the end of the week, although heavy fighting for local targets continued.

The enemy launched a concentrated attack against St. Lo in the 7th Army area on July 17. The bulges in the front line were taken back to the line north of St. Lo–Rampan–Le Mesnil Eury and thus prevented a breakthrough. St. Lo was abandoned to the enemy during the night of July 18/19, and the front was stabilized immediately south of the town. The enemy did not renew their heavy attacks here either, because of the heavy losses they had suffered.

We can expect the enemy's large-scale attacks from Caen, St. Lo and west of the Vire to be resumed as soon as more favourable weather conditions permit the unhampered use of the enemy air forces.

Units of the army and SS destroyed 2,117 enemy tanks and 345 aircraft between June 6 and July 23.

During the period June 6–July 23 our own losses were:

2,722	officers (including 10 generals,
	8 General Staff Officers, and 158 C.O.s)
110,337	NCOs and men
3,804	Russians
116,863	

Since June 6, 10,078 men have been brought in as replacements.

The disbandment of the 165th Reserve Division released 8,000 men for the infantry battalions which were sent to the front. Replacements for the SS panzer divisions are urgently needed.

Enemy strength and operational plans:
The enemy has at least 40 divisions and strong H.Q. troops in the landing area, and is still bringing in further troops and materials.

There are still 52 large troops formations in readiness in Great Britain, and of these about 42 could be transferred to the mainland.

The operational intentions of the Montgomery Army Group seem to be unchanged.

The British 2nd Army will attempt to force a breakthrough in the general direction of Falaise, thus preparing for a thrust on Paris.

The 1st American Army will endeavour to gain its first target, which is the extension of the land base as far as the line Domfront-Avranches.

We have no further reliable information as to the aim or the time of starting of the attack by the 1st American Army Group. With enemy forces being continually transferred to the Normandy front it is unlikely that there will be further landing operations at points very far distant from there, but the 15th Army sector from the north of the Somme to the Seine is still in great danger.

The more territory Montgomery gains to the south of the bridgehead, and the quicker he wins it, the less likelihood there is of the forces still in England effecting a new landing at another point. It is much more probable that in this case the British and Americans will feed all the reserves available into the bridgehead, and any fresh landings will probably only be affected by air landing troops south of the present bridgehead, so that they could then use their air landings on an operative basis.

Army Group B will continue the endeavour to prevent a further breakthrough. Some of the pressure at the battle front has been slightly eased by the appearance of the 326th and 363rd Divisions and the 116th Panzer Division, and now mobile forces can be released.

II Situation at sea:
Enemy destroyers and motor torpedo boats have been guarding the sea area off the landing beaches, and thus prevented our motor boats from attacking the landing fleets. Enemy naval forces are bombarding land targets in Normandy.

Supply traffic very active, coming from the recognized supply bases, Thames estuary, Portsmouth, Weymouth, Plymouth area, Bristol Channel, each sending one convoy daily to the bridgehead. Small convoys are arriving daily (L.C.T.).

The closing to French fishing fleets of the sea area Cap de la Hague–Alderney–St. Peter Port (Guernsey) to the south as far as the Breton coast, as reported on July 23, 1944, suggests enemy action to forestall the sending of supplies to the Chan-

A captured German pillbox on the Courseulles beach, shown on
July 14. Formerly house a German 88mm gun, it was now being used
as an Allied anti-aircraft post. The beach area was now used for
receiving the vital supplies and reinforcements needed to sustain
the invasion until the opening of Antwerp at the end of November.

nel Islands. There is a possibility of leapfrog landings on the
west coast of Cotentin.

There have been numerous small sea battles between our
protective naval forces and enemy motor boat fleets off the
coast between Dunkirk and Le Havre.

Most closely watched sea area around Brittany is off Brest.

Enemy mining activity continues to be slight.

III Situation in the air:
The enemy air forces were hindered by bad weather conditions, especially in the second half of the week.

Fighter and fighter-bomber formations gave strong support to the ground troops, covered the battle area, and attacked our troop movements in the rear areas. Fighter-bomber attacks against transport targets and airfields were carried as far afield as Brussels, Orleans and Nantes. Medium bomber formations turned their attention mainly against railway installations. They also attacked the Seine crossings and airfields.

Heavy bomber formations concentrated mainly on traffic centres north-east of Paris (Vaires Meaux, Laon, Tergnier, Ham, Chaulnes) and in the northern France-Belgium area (Maubeuge, Courtrai, Ghent, Alost) and also buildings and installations in V-1 launching sites and Luftwaffe ground organizations. About 2,200 heavy bombers were used to support the attack from the Orne bridgehead.

There has been complete air reconnaissance on the invasion front. Special points for this were Lille, St. Omer, both sides of the Somme, the Channel Islands, and the coasts of Brittany. Reconnaissance in depth against rail, road and sea traffic as far as Antwerp, Troyes and Angers.

IV Internal situation:

Behavior and attitude of the civilian population:
Unchanged—quiet and expectant.

Sabotage activity and Resistance organization:
Slight local decline in sabotage activities. We can expect further extension of the resistance organizations, especially in Belgium and north France, and in southern Brittany.

In Holland there have been further attacks on Dutch official buildings (including post offices) in the hope of obtaining rationed goods and stealing large sums of money.

Belgium and north France: increase in airborne supplies to secret agents (especially around St. Omer). On July 22, terrorists attacked the French national bank at Abbeville, stealing 39 million francs.

In Normandy, sabotage to cables, and small mines have been laid in the supply roads. In Brittany, the slight easing up of sabotage activities is, according to captured documents, a result of orders from the headquarters of the whole Resistance movement. Many supplies have been dropped in southern Brittany, so that in spite of present conditions, we can expect the arming and equipping of the Resistance movement to continue, and they will probably go over to a coordinated offensive. 88 terrorists have been shot and 65 taken prisoner.

V In detail:

Northern Military District:

A. *Coastal defenses (Alterations):*

(a) Organization of Defense: No change.

(b) Construction of Atlantic Wall:

Fortifications completed	1,291 positions ready for operation, 53 of them reinforced with concrete.
Approximate percentage of the whole project completed	71% completed, 3% reinforced with concrete.
Progress of construction and particular defects	July 14–20, 3 positions made ready for operation, 13 positions reinforced with concrete.
Labor employed	About 15,900 in fortress type and about 36,000 in field type construction.

(c) Consolidation of the land front: On the land front, digging in and the construction of obstacles continues.

B. *Enemy operations on the coast:*
None.

C. Operations of enemy aircraft:

(1) Number of raids:

Bombing raids	10 (5)
Strafing raids	7 (2)
Focal point of attacks	0 (0)

Total of attacks directed against:

Positions	2 (0)
Building sites	0 (0)
Airfields	2 (0)

(2) Casualties:

Soldiers killed	0 (0)
Soldiers wounded	0 (2)
German civilians killed	0 (0)
German civilians wounded	0 (0)
French civilians killed	10 (0)
French civilians injured	50 (1)

(3) Losses in material:

In attacks on transport targets	1 freighter with cargo slightly damaged, 4 locomotives put out of action, 2 buses and 1 truck badly damaged.

(4) Aircraft losses:

Enemy	42
Own	4

D.

(1) Feeling and behavior of the civilian population:
   No change.

(2) Instances of sabotage:

Attacks with use of explosives	2
Others	6 raids on Dutch public buildings and police.

15th Army H.Q.:

A. *Coastal defenses (Alterations):*

(a) Organization of Defense: Defense forces have been further weakened by the withdrawal of the 363rd Infantry Division and the 116th Panzer Division.

(b) Construction of Atlantic Wall:

Fortifications completed	2 anti-tank guns, 2 light gun positions, 1 pillbox. Shelters for personnel, munitions, supplies, horses, tanks, equipment and decontamination. Positions for light guns, anti-tank guns, anti-aircraft guns, mortars, machine guns, single-seat fighters, anti-tank mines and flame throwers, observation posts. Wiring and mining of foreshore obstacles, laying of minefields.
Approximate percentage of the whole project completed	Roughly 72%.
Progress of construction and particular defects	Shortage of building and obstacle materials (especially cement, wood, wire, mines and grenades), transport means, fuel, and labor.

Labor employed	(a) Soldiers: 20,445
	(b) Civilians: 18,792
	and 22 prisoners of war.

(c) Consolidation of the land front: Completed: Positions for infantry and anti-tank guns, anti-aircraft guns, cannon, mortars, close range anti-tank weapons and smoke mortars. Air raid shelters for arms stores, munitions, horses, supplies, kitchen staffs and personnel. Battle headquarters and tree shelter positions. Slit trenches, observation posts, dummy minefields, continued mining of the land at Le Havre, 1,024 anti-tank mines and 60 Teller mines have been laid. Air landing posts, and bringing up of mines and grenades.

B. Enemy operations on the coast:
   3.

C. Operations of enemy aircraft:

(1) Number of raids:

Bombing raids	72 (53)
Strafing raids	31 (16)
Focal point of attacks	Bomber formations: Bruges, Ghent, Antwerp, Brussels, Maubeuge, St. Quentin, Laon, Le Treport, Abbeville, St. Omer, Bethune, Albert, Montdidier, Neufchatel, St. Valery en Caux. Reconnaissance: Scheldt estuary, Brussels, Charleroi, St. Quentin, Soissons, Noyon, Amiens, Dieppe. Fighters and fighter-bombers: Scheldt estuary, Antwerp, Brussels, Charleroi, Charleville, Laon, Soissons, Rouen, Fecamp.

After repeated memos asking for more reinforcements and tanks,
Rommel was severely wounded when his car was strafed by Allied aircraft on July 17 near Vimoutiers. Von Kluge now took temporary
command of Army Group B, in addition to his post as C-in-C West,
and Rommel returned to his home in Herrlingen. He was forced to
commit suicide on October 14 after Hitler learned of his association
with the July 20 conspirators.

Total of attacks directed against:

Positions	16 (6)
Building sites	23 (23)
Transport targets	50 (24)
Airfields	10 (12)
Other targets	4 (4)

(2) Casualties:

Soldiers killed	67 (39)

Soldiers wounded	143 (30)
German civilians killed	2 (10)
German civilians wounded	1 (1)
French civilians killed	26 (13)
French civilians injured	71 (10)

Also many losses in French civilians killed and wounded without the exact figures known.

(3) Losses in material:

In attacks on positions	Destroyed: 1 searchlight, 2 radar installations—W.R.—(Würzburg Reise), 1 munition shelter (empty), 2 anti-aircraft batteries silenced. Damaged: 1 four-barrelled gun (2 cm.), 5 empty huts, 1 sound location equipment, armory, 1 hospital, railway lines, electricity and telephone cables. 1 shelter badly damaged (radar installation—Nordpol), roof collapsed in several places, and a large number of instruments shattered.
In attacks on buildings under construction	Badly damaged: 7 Moderately damaged: 2 Slightly damaged: 5.
In attacks on transport targets	Destroyed: 1 freight railway station, 3 industrial buildings, 3 locomotives (plus some more without exact figures being known), 59 railway cars (plus some more, exact number not known), 2 trucks, 1 dam. 1 canal lock (Oise-Aisne canal) unserviceable.

	Damaged: 10 industrial buildings, 4 railway bridges, 25 locomotives, 25 railway cars (plus many more, the exact number not known) railway tracks (very badly in parts), 7 trucks, telephone cable, 1 sound detector, and 1 railway anti-aircraft gun.
Unserviceable airfields	(Mons en Chaussee, Poix-Nord)
In attacks on airfields	Destroyed: 2 aircraft. Damaged: 1 aircraft, 2 runways, 1 tarmac, 1 set boundary lighting, hangars, telephone and electricity cables.
In other attacks	Destroyed: 2 trucks. Courtrai 25% destroyed, center of Rouen badly damaged, civilian losses high.

(4) Aircraft losses:

Enemy	18 (49) July 9–15, 1944.
Own	21 (31) July 8–14, 1944.

D.

(1) Feeling and behavior of the civilian population:

(2) Instances of sabotage:

Against railways	5
Against cables	7

Panzer Group West:
Main defense line, field type, built along the whole front.

7th Army H.Q.:

A. *Coastal defenses (Alterations):*

(a) Organization of Defense: The defense of Brittany has been further weakened by the removal of the 275th Infantry Division.

(b) Construction of Atlantic Wall: Available materials all used up. Coastal barriers have been strengthened by the erection of 484 cubic meters of steel reinforced concrete. No more supplies possible at the moment.

> For the Army Group High Command,
>
> The Chief of General Staff,
> Speidel

✠

ANALYSIS OF THE SITUATION, JULY 15, 1944

The position on the Normandy front is becoming daily increasingly difficult, and it is rapidly approaching its crisis.

Owing to the fierceness of the fighting, the enormous amount of material in the enemy's possession, especially their artillery and armor, and the undisputed mastery of the air obtained by the enemy air forces, our losses are so great that the battle potential of our divisions is rapidly deteriorating. Reinforcements from home come in very small quantities, and take weeks in arriving because of the bad transport situation. We have lost about 97,000 men, including 2,360 officers—which means an average loss of 2,500 to 3,000 men per day—and we have received until now 10,000 men as replacements, of which 6,000 have already been sent to the front.

Hitler survived the attempted assassination of July 20 at the Wolf's
Lair when the heavy wooden table shielded him from the blast. He
emerged more distrusting of his field commanders, and in the first
week of August, he overruled the advice of von Kluge and ordered a
major counterattack against the Allies. When Operation LÜTTICH
failed, Hitler blamed his "weak generals"—especially von Kluge—for
the failure. After being implicated in the July 20 plot, von Kluge
committed suicide on August 19.

Also the losses in supplies for the troops have been extraordinarily high, and it has not been possible to provide more
than very meagre replacements, as for example 17 tanks up till
now to replace about 225.

The divisions which have been newly brought in are not
used to battle conditions and with their small consignments of
artillery, anti-tank weapons, and means of engaging tanks in
close combat they are not able to offer effective resistance to
enemy large-scale attacks for any length of time, after being
subjected to concentrated artillery fire and heavy air raids for
hours on end. It has been proved in the fighting that even the
bravest unit is gradually shattered by the well-equipped enemy,
and loses men, weapons and territory.

The destruction of the railroad network, and the great danger of enemy air attacks on all the roads and paths for 150 kilometres behind the front has made the supply position so difficult that only the absolutely essential things could be brought up, and above all artillery and mortar ammunition was at a premium. These conditions are not likely to improve, as convoy vehicles are decreasing as a result of enemy action, and with the enemy capturing airfields in the bridgehead it can be expected that their air activities will increase.

No forces worth mentioning can be brought in to the Normandy front without weakening the 15th Army on the English Channel, or the Mediterranean front in southern France. The 7th Army front alone requires most urgently 2 fresh divisions, as the forces there are worn out.

The enemy are daily providing new forces and masses of materials for the front; the enemy supply lanes are not challenged by the Luftwaffe and enemy pressure is continually increasing.

In these circumstances it must be expected that the enemy will shortly be able to break through our thinly-held front, especially in the 7th Army sector, and push far into France. I should like to draw attention to the attached reports from the 7th Army and II Parachute Corps. Apart from local reserves of Panzer Group West, which are about to be sent to the Panzer Group's sector, and which in the face of the enemy air forces can only march during the night, there are no mobile reserves at all at our disposal to counter any breakthrough on the 7th Army front. Our own air force has hardly entered the battle at all as yet.

Our troops are fighting heroically, but even so the end of this unequal battle is in sight. In my view we should learn a lesson from this situation. I feel it is my duty as C. in C. of the Army Group to point this matter out.

(signed) Rommel

Appendix

(1) G.O.C. 7th Army reports orally on July 14:

"Our strength has sunk to such a low level that the local commanders can no longer guarantee their holding out against enemy large-scale attacks. Battle group of II Parachute Corps reports in addition that of the 1,000 men given to the 6th Parachute Regiment, 800 have become casualties in a very short time. The main reason for this was their lack of experience. Troops must first be trained by experienced soldiers behind the lines. However, the present conditions cannot be altered just yet, as we have no more reserves".

(2) Reports from 7th Army H.Q. dated July 15, on losses in personnel amongst the units under the command of G.H.Q. II Parachute Corps:

"3rd Parachute Division up till July 12—4,064 men
  Battle group 353rd Infantry Division (2 battalions) till July 12—485 men
  Battle group 266th Infantry Division (3 battalions) till July 12—316 men
  Battle group 343rd Infantry Division (1 battalion) till July 12—184 men

Since the battle strength of the units is sinking noticeably every day, as a result of the superior equipment of the enemy and their uninterrupted artillery fire, even the best troops are no longer in a condition to drive off for any length of time any attempts at a breakthrough".

(3) I should like to call your attention to the radio message from the battle group of II Parachute Corps on July 12 which was heard by C. in C. West.

✠

REVIEW OF THE SITUATION, JULY 19, 1944

The enemy were unsuccessful in their attempt to force an operational breakthrough during the $2\frac{1}{2}$ weeks of continuous fighting in western Normandy. They did however manage to achieve many local penetrations and to surround isolated pockets of our troops, which meant that our line had to be gradually withdrawn, and we were forced to surrender St. Lo.

The general course of the front line is not favourable, as the left wing is considerably in advance of the rest. The countryside helps our troops only in the northern sector.

Up till now we have found 13 to 14 enemy divisions, of which 2 are armored divisions. Of these, 6 infantry and 2 armored divisions are being used at the point of concentration of the attack, as are also several armored units and very heavy land artillery. As the enemy are only just starting their operations on the mainland, they have not yet marked out any boundaries for the bringing up of further supplies and reinforcements. The enemy have sufficient forces in the Normandy theater of operations to launch another large-scale attack very soon.

We have discovered that the enemy are regrouping on the northern front, and are moving their artillery to the southeast, bringing up more divisions (5 infantry and 4 armored divisions), and also they have started their attacks again on the transport routes behind our lines. There are further signs in their rear that they are preparing soon to begin a new attack to the south and south-west, concentrated on both sides of the Vire and Taute. Enemy attacks on both sides of the boundary of Panzer Group West will probably be continued.

We must also be prepared for a new onslaught with airborne landings, possibly combined with sea landings.

Our own troops are being hard pressed as a result of the heavy losses incurred in the defensive fighting. The battle potential of the infantry is being especially undermined by the artillery and mortar fire, which the enemy is putting up in hitherto unknown quantity, using a tremendous amount of ammunition (20:1), even for small reconnaissance raids, and for the large attacks this is increased to a 30 hour long pounding. Thus in prolonged fighting the potential of the infantry drops from that of a regiment to that of a company. Because of the losses incurred in the previous fighting, the infantry at the front line has become so depleted in many places that after similar artillery preparations, the enemy are bound to break through our lines. The defensive actions and counter-attacks which would then be necessary would quickly use up all the weak reserves in the division and corps. The Army's reserves at the moment consist of 3 battalions of the 275th Infantry Division.

The heavy artillery bombardments have led to a great loss in arms and equipment, which has been especially noticeable in radio equipment, artillery, cannon and machine guns.

The effect on morale of facing an enemy equipped with such superior weapons is especially bad when the commanders are killed and the units become mixed up in the desperate attempts to close up the gaps.

The use of the newly brought in battle group of the 275th Infantry Division and the 5th Parachute Division, cannot do much to help the difficulties of the 7th Army. These troops have had absolutely no training in field work or as a unit. Apart from the commanders themselves there are no experienced leaders or staffs in two regiments of the 5th Parachute Division. If they were to be used immediately in the danger areas, there would immediately be a crisis, and extremely heavy losses.

As a result of the increased interruptions on the railway lines and the insufficient motorized transport, the present impossible supply situation will only be improved if several munitions and fuel convoys can arrive. If the supply convoys cannot come, then we can expect the supply situation to deteriorate.

To strengthen the defense the Army should put the units and formations in order as far as the situation allows, and regroup the artillery at the danger points.

The following measures are absolutely essential:

(1) Bringing up as an army reserve a mobile formation, completely ready for battle, to be used west of the Vire

or to safeguard the boundary with Panzer Group West, (possibly also as defense against airborne or sea landings).

(2) The continual bringing up of reinforcements. At least 2 infantry battalions should be brought up every month, to reinforce each division, otherwise even the weak forces we have at our disposal up till now cannot be maintained.

(3) The strengthening of our front by the introduction of 1 to 2 mortar brigades, more heavy artillery, and replacing the cannon, trench mortars and machine guns which have been rendered useless.

(4) Increased supplies of munitions and fuel should be ensured to be brought in express trains, and the supply lines should be guarded by fighters and anti-aircraft guns, especially at the Loire bridges, which are a vital artery for the Army.

(5) Combating the particularly heavy artillery fire, and the raids by bombers and fighter bombers, by sorties of our own fighters, so that the attack on the morale of our troops can be effectively eased, if only for a time.

(signed) Hausser

✠

July 21, 1944

My Führer!

I forward herewith a report from Field Marshal Rommel, which he gave to me before his accident, and which has already been discussed with me.

I have now been here for about 14 days, and after long discussions with the responsible commanders on various fronts, especially the SS leaders, I have come to the conclusion that the Field Marshal was unfortunately right. Especially my conference yesterday with the commanders of units at

Caen, held just after the last heavy battle, forced me to the
conclusion that in our present position—considering the
material at our disposal—there is absolutely no way in which
we could do battle with the all-powerful enemy air forces, to
counter their present destructive activities, without being
forced to surrender territory. Whole armored units which had
been sent into the counter-attack, were attacked by terrific
numbers of aircraft dropping carpets of bombs, so that they
emerged from the churned-up earth with the greatest difficulty, sometimes only with the aid of tractors. And so they
were really too late when they arrived.

The psychological effect on the fighting forces, especially
the infantry, of such a mass of bombs, raining down on them
with all the force of elemental nature, is a factor which must
be given serious consideration. It is not in the least important
whether such a carpet of bombs is dropped on good or bad
troops. They are more or less annihilated by it, and above all
their equipment is ruined. It only needs this to happen a few
times and the power of resistance of these troops is put to the
severest test. It becomes paralyzed, dies; what is left is not
equal to the demands of the situation. Consequently the
troops have the impression that they are battling against an
enemy who carries all before him. This must make itself evi-
dent to an increasing extent.

I came here with the fixed intention of making effective
your order to make a stand <u>at any price</u>. But when one sees
that this price must be paid by the slow but sure destruction
of our troops—I am thinking of the Hitler Youth Division,
which has earned the highest praise—when one sees that the
reinforcements and replacements sent to all areas are nearly
always hopelessly inadequate, and that the armaments, especially artillery and anti-tank guns and the ammunition for
them, are not nearly sufficient for the soldiers' needs, so that
the main weapon in the defensive battle is the good spirits of
our brave men, then the anxiety about the immediate future
on this front is only too well justified.

I am able to report that the front has been held intact until now, due to the glorious bravery of our troops, and the determination of all commanders, especially the junior ones, although land has been lost daily.

However, in spite of all endeavours, the moment is fast approaching when this overtaxed front line is bound to break up. And when the enemy once reaches the open country a properly coordinated command will be almost impossible, because of the insufficient mobility of our troops. I consider it is my duty as the responsible commander on this front, to bring these developments to your notice in good time, my Fuehrer.

My last words at the Staff Conference south of Caen were:

"We must hold our ground, and if nothing happens to improve conditions, then we must die an honourable death on the battlefield".

(signed) von Kluge, Fieldmarshal

✠

TO ARMED FORCES HIGH COMMAND

In addition to my report to the Führer on July 21, I enclose the following summary of the situation by G.O.C. 7th Army, SS General Hausser.

I wish to add the following to measures suggested at the end of it.

to (1) Panzer Training Division to be relieved by the 363rd Division, which is coming up to the front, and placed under the command of the Army.

Length of time: 14 days.

2nd Panzer Division on the Army boundary to be relieved by the 326th Division. It cannot yet be decided whether they can be sent to the 7th Army or to the area of concentrated fighting around Caen.

to (2)   According to a message from Army G.H.Q. this will be impossible at the moment.

to (3)   The 7th, 8th and 9th Mortar Brigades are stationed at the centre of the present bitter fighting around Caen. Additional heavy artillery cannot at present be brought up, as the 14th Artillery Brigade amongst other units is being diverted to the east.

to (4)   Replacements of equipment are desired, although we cannot expect the amount required.

to (5)   We are attempting to engage the enemy, but with the enemy air superiority at the vital points on the front this has not yet been possible.

(signed) von Kluge, Fieldmarshal

CHAPTER 4

Operation COBRA and the Mortain Counteroffensive, July 24–August 7, 1944

At Army Group B headquarters, von Kluge expected the next Allied offensive to begin shortly near Caen. Operation FORTITUDE still kept the Germans in the dark as to Allied intentions and divided their strength between several fronts. To draw German attention away from the base of the Cotentin Peninsula, the Allies increased air reconnaissance around Caen, transferred British and U.S. warships to the Calais coast, and called upon the French underground to launch attacks in that same area. Von Kluge, however, was also watching Bradley's U.S. First Army in the St. Lô sector. He called Hausser at his Seventh Army HQ, ordering him to pull his tanks out of the front line and gather them in the rear as a reserve for a counterattack. German battle doctrine normally kept the armored units back as far as possible and near St. Lô, in the hedgerow country, infantry divisions would be more effective anyway. Hausser, however, ignored these orders, leaving Bayerlein's Panzer Lehr Division in place along the road from St. Lô to Périers. It would prove a very costly decision, as the U.S. Army was about to launch its COBRA breakout.

Operation COBRA began on July 25 with a massive carpet-bombing by 1,500 Flying Fortresses. Part of the assault was disrupted when bombs fell short on American troops, but Bayerlein's Panzer Lehr suffered tremendous losses under the bombardment. It now fell to the 2nd SS and 17th SS Panzer Divisions to fend off the American attack. Nineteen U.S. Army

divisions faced nine German divisions, many of them consisting mostly of "remnants" from other divisions.[1] The main
infantry divisions—the 243rd, 353rd, 91st Airlanding, and 5th
Parachute—were all seriously understrength. The Germans
had 110 tanks with which to counter 750 American Shermans.
Strongpoints all along the St. Lô line of resistance had been
wiped out, many of them by the sixty thousand Allied bombs
that were dropped in preparation for the advance. Furious
fighting broke out throughout the *bocage* as U.S. troops moved
inland. The ingenious invention of the "Rhinoceros"—steel
teeth welded to the front of the Shermans—made it possible
for the Americans to cut quickly through hedgerows that had
once presented a formidable barrier to their movement. They
now assembled fast, mobile columns of "Rhinos," bulldozers,
and engineer battalions to support the attack.[2] German tanks
and self-propelled guns, meanwhile, had to stay on or close to
the roads, but here they fell prey to Allied fighter-bombers.[3]

Near Caen, British and Canadian troops were sent against
Verrières Ridge, an effort which prevented large numbers of
German forces from moving westward to the U.S. front.
Although Montgomery dreamed of a breakthrough in this sector, the battle for Verrières soon broke down in the face of
fierce German opposition, with the defenders holding firm on
the ridge and in defensive positions located in the villages and
farms beyond.

The American breakout pushed forward with even greater
energy. On July 27 Périers fell at last to the American assault,
and Coutances was overrun the next day. Von Kluge called
Jodl at Rastenburg to warn that the front had collapsed into a
wild mêlée of fighting, the only German resistance being
offered by isolated bands of exhausted, dispirited, and con-
fused soldiers. They were pursued relentlessly by a surge of
American tank and infantry forces, which were constantly
being refreshed by the arrival of reinforcements. Hitler
authorized von Kluge to pull a few divisions away from the Fif-

---

[1] Keegan, 232.
[2] Blumenson, 206–7; Weigley, 149.
[3] Overy, 171.

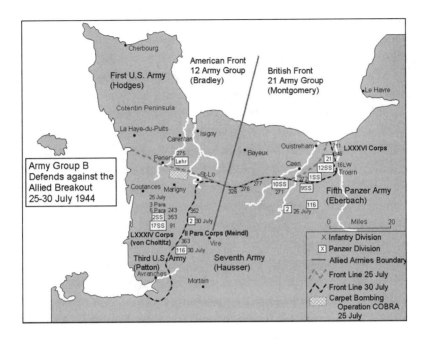

teenth Army in the Pas de Calais and rush them to Normandy to help stem the American tide.[4] Most of the Channel forces, however, were still required to remain in place, just in case the Allies launched an amphibious operation against the V-1 launching sites. On July 28, General George S. Patton arrived in Normandy to take command of the U.S. Third Army, leaving behind his forty-five fictitious FUSAG divisions in southeast England. His name alone had a significant impact upon German morale, standing as it did for his extraordinary offensive spirit and his ability to drive his soldiers to the limits of their endurance during offensive operations.[5]

The American forces now split and went their separate ways. Patton's VIII Corps, under Middleton, began a rapid drive through Brittany, heading toward Rennes and Brest. Lying before him, the interior of Brittany was almost empty of German troops, who had either already left for Normandy or were concentrating on the Atlantic coast for the defense of its ports. Anxious to make up for lost time, Patton was able to

---

[4] Gilbert, 557.

[5] Keegan, 235.

cross the hundred-mile base of Brittany in four days. Meanwhile, the U.S. First Army maintained its pressure against
Hausser's Seventh Army. Things were happening so fast that
von Kluge was having trouble keeping pace with events. Signals to Hausser demanding information remained unan-
swered. By July 30, the Americans had "turned the corner" at
Avranches, and back at the Wolf's Lair, Jodl wrote: "I have
advised the Führer of the imminent fall of Avranches. He
reacted favorably to the idea of the eventual withdrawal from
France." Jodl called Blumentritt at St. Germain, telling him in
guarded terms to be prepared for a withdrawal from France.
Warlimont was designated OKW liaison with von Kluge's headquarters as it prepared for the mass withdrawal, with instructions to watch over von Kluge, who since the July 20 plot had
fallen under a cloud of suspicion. On July 31, von Kluge signaled his doubt that the enemy could still be stopped. He gave
a brief assessment of the situation: "It's a madhouse here!"[6]

The initial success of COBRA encouraged Montgomery to
try for an accompanying British breakout on the Caen front.
Operation BLUECOAT made slow progress initially but eventually succeeded in keeping the 9th SS Panzer pinned to the
Caumont area and thus unable to reinforce the Mortain zone.
To the west, U.S. tanks were spearheading the advance at
Brécey and Avranches, forcing Hitler to concede that France,
not Russia, was now the focal point of the war. The Führer
remained in charge of all strategic and tactical positions. He
halted further construction on the Atlantic Wall north of the
battlefront and shifted these crews to the construction of rearward defense lines. At the same time, Anglo-American
bombers were pounding von Aulock's forces in the old citadel
at St. Malo, where the garrison remained under Hitler's orders
to fight to the last man.

Taking up his mission of watching over von Kluge, Warlimont was stunned to learn on August 2 that Hitler had
changed his mind: there would be no withdrawal.[7] Instead, the

---

[6] Blumeson, 323.
[7] Keegan, 240.
[8] Keegan, 241.

Führer ordered a counterattack from the area east of Avranches, aiming to re-establish positions on the coast and so once more close the ring in southern Normandy. With his forces being rapidly depleted, and with no hope of reinforcement, Hitler now declared, "We must wheel north like lightning and turn the entire enemy front from the rear."[8]

With these latest orders, Warlimont arrived at St. Germain carrying plans for Operation LÜTTICH, the brainchild of Hitler in which a minimum of four panzer divisions would attack westward at Mortain and then push on toward Avranches and the coast. This move would trap Patton's Third Army in Brittany. When the messenger arrived at St. Germain, von Kluge was at Seventh Army HQ at Le Mans trying desperately to halt the American breakthrough, so Warlimont conferred with Blumentritt instead. The Army Group B Chief of Staff became totally enraged by the plan. Since D-Day, the Seventh Army had lost 750 of 1,400 tanks, plus 160,000 killed, wounded, or taken prisoner out of the 450,000 troops prior to the invasion. A top-secret signal from Hitler arrived for von Kluge: Army Group B with all its main armored units would prepare a counteroffensive aimed at breaking through to Avranches, with the objective of isolating the enemy forces and ensuring their destruction.[9]

On August 3, General Warlimont then flew to meet Eberbach and Dietrich to give them the plans for Operation LÜTTICH, the Mortain counteroffensive. Dietrich warned Warlimont of the consequences of pulling SS divisions away from Caen: "It's madness, sheer madness. We shall run into a trap!" The three commanders considered the plan absurd,[10] but it was, however, a direct order from the Führer and had to be obeyed. On that same day, the American forces entered Mortain. Meanwhile, the Germans were tenaciously battling Montgomery's forces near Caen and a second American force at Vire. Seeing new possibilities in the campaign, Bradley ordered Patton to halt his drive into Brittany, a major revision of the original OVERLORD plan, and instead turn east with all

---

[9] Copp, 190.
[10] Stacey, 213.

available strength in an attempt to encircle the Seventh Army.[11] Dietrich was not the only commander who could see the emerging trap.

German misgivings aside, preparations for Operation LÜT-TICH were now underway. The 89th Infantry Division from the Fifteenth Army relieved the *Leibstandarte* 1st SS Panzers so that they could join the counterattack at Mortain. Warlimont informed Hitler that everyone was confident of success. ULTRA, however, intercepted von Kluge's warning that the counterattack would end in disaster, along with Hitler's reply to "Proceed as ordered." Bletchley Park relayed these messages to Churchill in London. The night before the attack began, Montgomery and Bradley were alerted to the westward movement of enemy panzer divisions.[12]

Von Kluge had no choice but to go ahead as ordered. After the failure of the July 20 plot, no battlefield commander would dare to question orders or suggest retreat. To make matters worse, von Kluge, like Rommel, had been aware of the assassination plot and was, to some extent at least, implicated in it. Before his own death, a delirious von Stülpnagel had unwittingly betrayed others.[13] The only escape for von Kluge was to play the role of the loyal subordinate. He pressed on at full speed in his preparations for the counterattack, knowing that it was his forces that would pay the price.

The 116th, 2nd, 2nd SS, and 1st SS Panzer divisions, the last newly-arrived from the Caen sector, all moved toward Mortain. By August 6 they were in position. Hitler now called upon von Kluge, uncharacteristically, to delay the attack. The Führer wanted to add the 9th, 11th, 9th SS, and 10th SS Panzer divisions so that, with eight panzer divisions abreast, they could inflict a defeat upon the Allies from which they could never recover.[14] Four days earlier, von Kluge would have welcomed the news of reinforcement, but now the tactical situation had

---

[11] Omar Bradley, *A Soldier's Story* (New York: Random House, 1999), 363–65.
[12] D'Este, 417.
[13] Müller, "Witzleben, Stülpnagel, and Speidel," in Barnett, ed., 64.
[14] Keegan, 245.

changed for the worse. American spearheads were driving towards Le Mans, threatening the envelopment of his forces between the Americans in the south and the British to the north of Caen. The British and Canadian forces were pressing so hard in this area that it was inconceivable that the 9th and 10th SS could reach the gathering area near Mortain. Weighing these factors, von Kluge stated that his own preparations were too advanced to change.

Learning of the impending counterattack fours hours before it began,[15] Montgomery and Bradley quickly realized the enormity of the German decision. The enemy was intending to send the Seventh and the Fifth Panzer Armies into a salient. Should the Allies succeed in closing the gap between the American position at Argentan and the British one near Falaise, von Kluge's two armies could be encircled and destroyed. At Le Mans, Hausser readied his troops for the impending battle, even though he was personally convinced that Operation LÜTTICH would end in disaster. "On the successful execution of the operation the Führer has ordered," he told them, "depends the decision of the war itself." The attack began at midnight, though on a much smaller scale than Hitler had planned. No artillery barrage preceded the attack, as the Germans hoped to heighten the element of surprise when they began their advance down narrow corridors towards Avranches.

The southern columns did achieve some success, but the American troops soon recovered from the surprise and dug in, bringing the forward movement of the 2nd SS to a halt. The northern German column was not opposed by American forces in such strength and might have been expected to make better progress. Hausser tried to call in the 116th Panzer Division, which should have entered the fray already, but its commander, von Schwerin, insisted that he was too hard-pressed where he stood to take the risk of disengaging. This may have concealed an unwillingness to act, for von Schwerin had lost faith in eventual victory. His 116th Panzers had never crossed their start lines because von Schwerin withheld the orders

---

[15] D'Este, 417, 420.

from his subordinates. Hausser subsequently relieved him of his command for dereliction of duty.

Events everywhere were turning against the German forces. The Mortain counteroffensive was bogging down. Hitler ordered von Kluge to remove the Eberbach forces from Caen to Mortain. In Brittany, U.S. troops were closing in on the ports of Brest, St. Malo, Nantes, Lorient, and St. Nazaire. Operation COBRA had destroyed nearly thirteen German divisions, inflicting 250,000 casualties. On the British-Canadian front, Operation TOTALIZE was in planning, an attempt to drive southward and break out of the old GOODWOOD corridor and capture the high ground outside Falaise.

Near Paris, Allied combat air patrols had established a barrier around the runways of the Luftwaffe's Third Air Fleet, preventing any of its three hundred promised fighters from reaching the Mortain area.[16] American medium bombers were now engaging pinpoint targets while British Typhoon fighters flew almost three hundred sorties against the 2nd Panzer Division. In spite of these difficulties, Hitler ordered Operation LÜTTICH to be prosecuted with reckless abandon.

By August 8, Operation LÜTTICH had failed. Victory went to the American defenders, who refused to be driven from their main line of resistance and even regained some of the territory lost in the initial German onslaught. If von Kluge had hoped the attack might help prove his loyalty to Hitler, it had done him little good when the Führer blamed him for its failure: "The attack failed because Kluge wanted it to fail," Hitler told Warlimont.[17] Ahead of them now lay the struggle to preserve what remained of the German army in Normandy, which was now in mortal danger of being encircled in the fields west of Falaise.

✠

---

[16] Keegan, 247.
[17] Keegan, 248.

WEEKLY REPORT, JULY 24–30, 1944

I Estimate of the situation as a whole.

The week was characterized by the large-scale attack by the 1st American Army, which was probably reinforced by units of the 3rd American Army (see below).

On July 25 and 26, 2 Canadian infantry divisions with 1 armored brigade attempted to force a breakthrough along a 7 km. front in the sector of Panzer Group West between Bourguebus and the Orne. I SS Panzer Corps, after hard fighting and counter-attacks, successfully drove off the attack, and the enemy halted in the face of the infantry of Panzer Group West; the artillery fire continued in intensity. The introduction of fresh infantry and tanks has been noticed daily in the area south of Caen.

On July 30 the enemy attacked on the western wing of Panzer Group West, and forced a bridgehead 5 km. deep and 8 km. wide. The battle in the area south of Caumont is continuing.

The expected enemy attack on the 7th Army began on July 24. Following an artillery barrage and carpet bombing of unprecedented intensity the enemy succeeded, after a day's heavy fighting, in breaking through the front between the Vire and the sea. Our losses in men and materials were so high because of the enemy's superiority in artillery and the air that it was not possible to build up a new defense front quickly. Although we managed to stop the enemy large-scale attack between the Army boundary and Percy, the position between the St. Hilaire–Percy line and the sea is still not clear, and strong enemy forces are being brought into the gap.

The enemy will continue their push to the south, and also intend to attack on a broad front in the Panzer Group West sector.

During the period June 6–July 30, units of our army and the SS destroyed 2,395 enemy tanks and 402 aircraft.

Our own losses for the period June 6–July 27 were:

3,017	officers (including 11 generals, 8 general staff officers, and 180 C.Os.)
120,424	NCOs and men
3,806	Russians
127,247	Total

Since June 6, 14,594 men have been brought in as replacements.

Enemy strengths and operational intentions

It still seems improbable that the enemy will attempt a further landing on the west coast of Europe. A further American-Canadian High Command has been transferred to Normandy, and probably 2 army groups have been formed. Now that Cherbourg is being used more and more, we can expect them to bring in extra forces to a greater extent.

The enemy now have about 45 divisions and strong forces of G.H.Q. troops in the landing area. They could bring in at least 35 divisions of the 45 in Great Britain, and they will probably transfer more troops from the U.S.A.

The British and American forces will first attempt to extend their land base further south, and if this breakthrough is successful they will turn the mass of their troops against Paris. In addition the Americans will strive to cut off Brittany from the land.

A large-scale landing by airborne troops south of the present bridgehead can be expected to ensure the success of the new operations.

Army Group B will attempt to prevent a breakthrough even though it means the reckless exposure of the lines hitherto not attacked. However, the lack of tanks and other fast moving units is telling against the highly mobile enemy.

II Situation at sea.

Enemy destroyers, gunboats and fleets of speedboats are keeping a close watch on the sea areas off the landing area.

The enemy are keeping their bridgehead continually supplied. Convoys sailing in and out of Cherbourg were noticed for the first time on July 26. A small amount of unloading activity has apparently begun at the large and small harbours. There is still no shipping in the inner harbour, according to our air reconnaissance.

We are still able to bring small amounts of supplies to the Channel Islands as planned. On July 28/29 a convoy was intercepted by strong formations of fighter bombers between St. Malo and Jersey.

There has been only slight speedboat and air activity off the Dutch coast.

There is armed enemy reconnaissance in the area between Calais and Belle Ile whenever the weather permits. Our escort vessels have had several encounters with enemy motor torpedo boats in the sea area between Fecamp and Le Havre.

There have been numerous fighter-bomber attacks on our escort vessels between Ostend and Le Havre.

The enemy sea control off Brittany is as usual centred on Brest. Little enemy mining activity.

III Situation in the air.

Most of the enemy air forces in the battle area were employed in the support of ground troops west of the Vire. (They were using 1,500 4-engined and 400 twin-engined aircraft, and also about 3,000 fighters and fighter-bombers on the second day of the attack).

Apart from that there have been continual heavy attacks on transport targets and the telephone systems.

Strong forces of enemy fighters and fighter-bombers supported their ground troops, and prevented our air force from reaching the battle area. They also raided targets as far as Rheims, Orleans, transport in the Loire estuary, Seine crossings, and airfields.

Medium bomber formations attacked for the most part railway installations, especially in the area enclosing Paris, Chartres, Argentan and Lisieux. Heavy forces made a raid on the bridges near Tours.

For 2 days heavy bomber formations dropped bombs in quantities previously unknown on the main defense line in the area immediately behind the line west of St. Lo. Before the offensive began west of the Vire there were heavy raids on the airfields of Athies, Juvencourt, Creil, Beaumont, (all north-east of Paris).

There has been complete reconnaissance in the battle area and to the rear of it, as far as the weather would permit. Pyrotechnic devices were again used to guard the Seine crossings at night. Heaviest concentration north of the Seine in the area Nieuport–Le Treport–Amiens–St. Pol–Lille.

IV Internal situation

Attitude of the civilian population is expectant; enemy successes sometimes openly acclaimed.

Sabotage activity and Resistance organizations:

Another increase in sabotage activities. The activities of the Resistance organizations are becoming more military in character, especially in Brittany.

There have been further raids on municipal and postal buildings in Holland, increased sabotage activity in Belgium and France; in Normandy more sabotage and attacks, and in Brittany, further attacks on enemy vehicles. Having abandoned their temporary armed peace, the Resistance organizations have gone over to miniature warfare. The methods of carrying out raids and the safeguarding of Maquis camps with minefields suggest they have military leadership. Continued supplying by air leads us to believe that the Resistance movement will increase its activities. 71 terrorists have been shot, and 51 taken prisoner.

Northern Military District:

A. Coastal defenses (Alterations):

(a) Organization of Defense: Unchanged.

(b) Construction of Atlantic Wall:

Fortifications completed	1,321 positions ready for use, 33 reinforced with concrete.
Approximate percentage of the whole project completed	73% completed, 2% also reinforced with concrete.
Progress of construction and particular defects	July 21–27, 30 positions ready for use, 10 positions reinforced with concrete.
Labor employed	No change.

(c) Consolidation of the land front: Ground obstacles in the land front have been laid.

B. Enemy operations on the coast:
    None.

C. Operations of enemy aircraft:

(1) Number of raids:

Bombing raids	2 (10)
Strafing raids	12 (7)
Focal point of attacks	0 (0)

Total of attacks directed against:

Positions	0 (2)
Building sites	0 (0)
Transport targets	10 (8)
Airfields	2 (2)

(2) Casualties:

Soldiers killed	0 (0)
Soldiers wounded	0 (0)
German civilians killed	0 (0)
French civilians killed	4 (10)
French civilians injured	12 (50)

(3) Losses in material:

In attacks on transport targets	2 ships, 7 locomotives damaged.
In other attacks	Main transformer of Huitzen transmitter burnt out, transmitter out of action.

(4) Aircraft losses:

Enemy	1
Own	10

D.

(1) Feeling and behavior of the civilian population: Negative.

(2) Instances of sabotage:

Against railways	1
Against cables	2
Against crops	0
Against soldiers	0
Attacks with use of explosives	0
Cases of arson	1

15th Army H.Q.:

A. *Coastal defenses (Alterations):*

(a) Organization of Defense: Defensive dispositions greatly weakened by the withdrawal of the 84th and 331st Infantry Divisions.

(b) Construction of Atlantic Wall:

Fortifications completed	Fortress type: positions for 2 guns, 2 anti-tank guns, 1 anti-aircraft gun, 9 light guns, 1 pillbox, 1 battle headquarters, 1 command headquarters, 1 double machine gun casemate, 1 triple embrasure tower, 2 fire control positions. Field type: Positions for light guns, anti-tank guns, mortars, flame-throwers, tank mines, searchlights, observation posts, air raid shelters for men, munitions, dummy installations. More beach obstacles have been completed.
Approximate percentage of the whole project completed	About 83%.
Progress of construction and particular defects	According to plan. Main shortages are cement, building materials, mines, and above all, fuel.
Labor employed	(a) Soldiers: 17,538 (b) Civilians: 23,796 and 22 prisoners of war.

(c) Consolidation of the land front: Completed—positions
    for guns, anti-tank guns, mortars, machine guns, air raid
    shelters for men and munitions, observation posts. The
    building of obstacles for airborne landings is continuing,
    1,024 anti-tank mines and 60 Teller mines have been laid,
    and there is mining at the fortress of Le Havre.
        Construction is slowed down because of the shortages
    as under (3) (b).

C. Operations of enemy aircraft:

(1) Number of raids:

Bombing raids	66 (72)
Strafing raids	60 (31)
Focal point of attacks	Bomber formations: Gravelines-Ghent-Brussels-Valenciennes-Cambrai-Arras-Aire. Abbeville–Amiens–Laon–Chauny–Chateau Thierry–Creil–Dieppe. Reconnaissance: St. Pol–Amiens–Le Treport–Lille–Nieuport. Fighters and fighter-bombers: Terneuzen–Macheln–Huy–Charleroi–Rathel–Gisors–Cap d'Antifer.

Total of attacks directed against:

Positions	8 (16)
Building sites	18 (23)
Transport targets	76 (50)
Airfields	11 (10)
Other targets	13 (4)

(2) Casualties:

Soldiers killed	50 (67)
Soldiers wounded	71 (143)
German civilians killed	3 (2)
German civilians wounded	— (1)
French civilians killed	21 (26)
French civilians injured	28 (71)

(3) Losses in material:

In attacks on positions	Destroyed: 1 barrack hut, 1 accommodation building, 1 ammunition store, 1 machine gun, 1 cannon. Also in attacks on Luftwaffe fuel stores: an oil and grease distribution centre burnt out, 2 barracks huts destroyed, 3,000 liters auto fuel and tank wood burnt up. Damaged: 1 anti-aircraft position, 2 cannon.
In attacks on buildings under construction	Destroyed: 2. Badly damaged: 4. Moderately damaged: 4. Slight damage: 2.
In attacks on transport targets	Destroyed: 1 railway installation, 27 locomotives, 92 railway cars (of which 45 were blown up with ammunition), 25 trucks, 1 coal crane, 2 cannon (2 cm.), 1 street bridge, 1 ship. Damaged: 15 industrial buildings, 1 railway bridge, 1 water tower, 20 locomotives, 80 railway cars, 1 crane, 3 trucks, 1 omnibus, 2 ships, 2 trucks blown up by mines.

Unserviceable airfields	Athies.
In attacks on airfields	<u>Destroyed</u>: 2 berths, 1 airport building, 1 air control centre, 1 direction finder, 500 rounds 8.8 ammunition. <u>Damaged</u>: 7 airfields, 9 runways, 4 tarmacs, 1 airfield building, 1 set boundary lighting, 1 tarmac road, pipes.
In other attacks	<u>Destroyed</u>: 50 houses. <u>Damaged</u>: 3 industrial installations.

(4) Aircraft losses:

Enemy	32 (July 16–22, 1944) (18).
Own	37 (July 15–21, 1944) (21).

D.

(1) Feeling and behavior of the civilian population:

(2) Instances of sabotage:

Against railways	4
Against cables	3

Panzer Group West:

Defense greatly weakened since the 2nd and 116th Panzer Divisions were removed.

7th Army H.Q.:

Brittany: Defense greatly weakened by the removal of the remains of the 5th Parachute Division. Field fortress building on the coast continued. Lack of cement and concrete continues to hamper building.

For the Army Group High Command,

The Chief of General Staff,
Speidel

WEEKLY REPORT, JULY 31–AUGUST 7, 1944

Estimate of the situation

In the landing area the enemy have already at least 46 divisions and strong forces of H.Q. troops; in addition they could bring another 35 divisions from Great Britain, and more from the U.S.A. We judge from the amount of transport being brought across the Channel that they are probably bringing 4 divisions across each week.

It still appears that the enemy intend to make a push for Paris. To this end the British forces are attempting to win area around Falaise, and the American troops are trying to cut off the 7th Army in the Normandy area and occupy the Le Mans sector.

The British also intend to continue their attempts at a breakthrough at the Vire, although concentration of forces east of the Orne and other reports lead us to believe that they will attack from this area from the north to south, with the idea of encircling us.

Parts of the American forces are intended to seal off Brittany and occupy the province.

The extending of the enemy operations and the forces involved in such an action make it seem unlikely that they will attempt a second big landing operation on the west coast of Europe, although they may try to land airborne troops behind our lines to open up the road to Paris.

In more than 2 months of fighting the 5th Panzer Army and the 7th Army opposing a vastly superior enemy have caused the failure of his first operational plan. Only now has the enemy succeeded in capturing Cotentin, thus coming nearer to his first targets on the western side: the line Domfront-Avranches, cutting off Brittany.

All units available have been sent from Army Group B to the front line, and the armored units have been assembled on the western flank of the 7th Army so that with the east-to-west push to Avranches they could cut off the enemy in Cotentin, thus making impossible further operations to the south.

The shortage of armored and fast moving units compared with the highly mobile enemy forces is still serious. Because of the enemy superiority in materials, especially in the air our losses have been high, although units of the army and the SS have shot up 2,799 enemy tanks and 450 aircraft since June 6.

From June 6 to August 6 our losses have been:

3,219	officers (including 14 generals, 9 general staff officers, 201 C.Os.)
141,046	other ranks
3,810	Russians
148,075	Total

Replacements arrived: 19,914 men
On the way: 16,457 men

                              36,371 men

For the Army Group High Command,

The Chief of General Staff,
Speidel

✠

TO C.-IN-C. WEST, AUGUST 7, 1944

Below is submitted an extract from a report from 7th Army H.Q. submitted at 0350 hours on August 7, SS General Hausser has given spoken approval to this draft.

"Part II:

State of the troops in the rear zone:

As a result of a breakthrough by enemy tanks at the left end of the front, most of the divisions (77th, 91st, 275th, units of the 265th, units of the 353rd, 5th Parachute, 2nd SS Panzer, and 17th SS Panzer Grenadier Divisions) which have been fighting all the time from the start of the invasion without any rest and with few supplies reaching them, are all split up into small groups. They have fought their way separately back through the enemy lines. Groups of men, mostly without officers or N.C.O.s with them, are wandering aimlessly through the countryside in a general easterly or south-easterly direction, some following express instructions to rally there, and some following wild report of their orders. They are mostly heading for Bagnoles and Le Mans.

Most of these straggling groups are in a very bad condition. They are bringing only a part of their arms with them (only guns, revolvers and Tommy guns). Motorized and cavalry units still have a few machine guns and heavy infantry weapons, although most of them are in need of repair. Their clothing is in a terrible state. Many are without headgear and belt, and have worn out their boots. Many are going barefooted. Where they cannot obtain food from supply stores they are living off the country with no respect for property, and the hatred of the civil population and the terrorist activities are thus intensified. The terrorists have wiped out a considerable number of them. The parachute troops are especially unpopular with the people.

The morale of these straggling forces is badly shaken. The enemy command of the air has contributed largely to this, as it makes it impossible to steer a straight course by day in the difficult countryside. In addition there is the enemy superiority in tanks and heavy weapons of all kinds, and his greater supplies of ammunition. The troops have had no proper rations for weeks. There is no radio apparatus available. Newspapers never reach the men, although the enemy produces daily "News for the troops" ["Nachrichten für die Truppe"], which is cleverly written, and is being dropped in great numbers from enemy aircraft. Such a state of affairs cannot be endured by even the best troops for any length of time without having an unfortunate effect. In addition, rumors are being circulated by enemy agents: the second attempt to murder the Führer and Himm-

ler has been successful—the Russians have entered Germany—
it is useless to continue the war, you have already lost it—why
not go home and not sacrifice your life at the last minute for a
lost cause.

It must be stated that the greater part of the stragglers are
trying to return to their former division. The rounding-up staff
of the Army H.Q. has been set up to collect all the stragglers
and maintain discipline in the rear areas. To this staff have
been assigned a battle and a transport commander. The following have been placed at their disposal: a fortification engineers
commander with road repair squads, army and combined
forces patrols, military police forces, special duty patrols from
the Army H.Q. and at the moment 2 mobile field courts mar-
tial, and another is to be added later. All stragglers are to be
held up at a special line, collected in reception camps, and
formed into replacement units to be sent immediately back to
the front line."

G.H.Q., Army Group B

CHAPTER 5

Encirclement in the Falaise Pocket, August 8–August 21, 1944

Operation LÜTTICH, the German counterattack at Mortain, was running out of steam by August 8, and von Kluge now reported to OKW that "the idea of the thrust to Avranches is scarcely feasible." To the east, British and Canadian troops were already astride the Caen-Falaise highway preparing for a new offensive aimed at the encirclement of two German armies in the Falaise pocket. The Canadian attack, Operation TOTALIZE, began with a massive aerial bombardment by one thousand RAF heavy bombers on the evening of August 7. That night, the Canadians began their advance under the cover of darkness, but although they achieved some initial successes, the attack soon broke down into confusion. The following day, a second wave of bombers from the U.S. Eighth Air Force targeted the German 89th "Horseshoe" Division. Unfortunately, a number of their bombs fell short, landing in the First Canadian Army gathering area. The Polish Armored Division and the 3rd Canadian Infantry Division suffered more than three hundred casualties in these short-bombings,[1] but the devastation was far worse on the German side: the 89th Division was virtually destroyed by the bombing and the Canadian attack that followed. As the remnants of this shattered formation fell back, they were integrated into battle groups of the 12th SS and put back into the line.

With the failure of LÜTTICH, the Fifth Panzer and Seventh Armies began to retreat from the dangerous pocket into which

---

[1] Stacey, 223.

they had advanced. The Germans now had nineteen divisions concentrated along the edge of the original bridgehead between the Orne and Vire Rivers. Bradley's forces—the U.S. First Army under General Hodges and Patton's Third Army—were to the west and south, respectively. The British and Canadians stood to the north, now joined by two émigré formations, the 1st Polish and the 2nd Free French armored divisions. With the emergence of the "pocket," the Germans were in grave danger of becoming trapped, and Montgomery now agreed to shift the boundary line between the American and British forces. A fourteen-mile gap existed between Falaise and Argentan, which Montgomery proposed would be sealed by British forces over the next few days. In the Mortain area, Eberbach's Fifth Panzers suffered devastating attacks by Allied warplanes. Hundreds of tanks, trucks, artillery pieces, supply wagons, and anti-tank guns were destroyed in the barrage. Despite utter chaos at the front, in Berlin, the main focus remained largely on rounding up conspirators, eight of whom were hanged on August 8.

Von Kluge sent a message to Jodl at the Wolf's Lair on August 10 asking permission to temporarily withdraw Eberbach's panzer group from Mortain and use it to halt the American attack northward towards Alençon. His request amounted to nothing less than an abandonment of Operation LÜTTICH, but von Kluge backed this up with a statement that all the generals under his command agreed that the withdrawal was necessary.[2] Dietrich, Hausser, and Eberbach had not been tarred with the same brush as von Kluge, and were not suspected of having any connection to the conspiracy. Von Kluge hoped that their support would remove the taint of disloyalty from his request to withdraw. Bletchley Park monitored these messages and eagerly awaited Hitler's reply. Hitler either ignored this request or was shielded from the truth by his staff at OKW. He remained unmoved by the exhaustion of his troops, the battered state of their equipment, and the inability of his commanders to make large-scale troop movements during the

---

[2] Weigley, 203; Stacey, 246.

daylight hours owing to overwhelming Allied airpower. Hitler's personal command also caused delays, as it prevented his commanders from taking immediate action in the field or responding to changing situations. It often required twenty-four hours for Hitler to digest recommendations and return instructions to the field commanders.

The determination of the German army in the field, however, was still able to produce results and offer tenacious resistance to the Allied advance. The Canadians of Operation TOTALIZE were brought to a grinding halt once the defenders recovered from their initial losses. Artillery and aircraft could not restore the initiative. Fighter bombers were at the mercy of the weather. On August 11, Montgomery issued new directives to his commanders. General Simonds' II Canadian Corps was to seize Falaise and continue on to the British Second Army sector towards Argentan.[3] This involved an eight-mile advance through an area where the Canadians were already struggling to push onwards after an exhausting three-day battle with no reinforcements. The American Third Army, on the other hand, had fresh troops from two armored and two infantry divisions, with most of the Third Army as backup. Why Montgomery did not use this force to close the Falaise Gap still remains an issue for debate.[4]

The German forces now fighting for their lives at Mortain received orders and counter-orders from Hitler regarding the conduct of the battle. St. Barthélémy and Mortain soon fell to U.S. forces. Hitler's all-out plunge for Avranches had not only been halted; the Americans had regained lost territory. Von Kluge once again met with Generals Hausser, Dietrich, and Eberbach, and called Jodl to say that the Avranches offensive was no longer possible.[5] He realized that his counterattack, always thought of by Hitler as the great offensive to turn the battle, had failed. He had only mustered four divisions instead of the expected eight. Fresh divisions arriving from throughout France found themselves being mauled by Allied aircraft

---

[3] Weigley, 203.

[4] D'Este, 437–60; Copp, 218–20.

[5] OKW, 84–86; Weigley, 203.

while en route. Von Kluge realized he must get permission to withdraw his troops from the salient before the remnants of Fifth Panzer and Seventh Armies were trapped. Receiving the needed permission by late evening, von Kluge signaled to his subordinate commanders: "The Seventh Army will withdraw from the Mortain salient tonight."

By late afternoon of August 12, long convoys of horse-drawn wagons, vehicles, and men were streaming east to escape what would be called the Falaise pocket. Allied aircraft strafed these miserable caravans and pounded them with rockets and bombs. To assist the withdrawal, Eberbach organized a defense at Argentan composed of the 116th and 2nd Panzer Divisions, along with sixty tanks from the *Leibstandarte* division. Bradley, for his part, ordered a halt to the U.S. advance as they were already beyond the Carrouges-Sées stop line, which marked the division between the British and American area of operations. Patton was livid. If the Germans were ordered to stay at Avranches with the bulk of their armor, he believed his army could slice behind the two German armies and trap them. Swift action could close the pocket, but Bradley refused.[6] Eisenhower agreed. Bradley felt Patton's army itself could become trapped in the narrow neck of the pocket—the Falaise Gap—through which thousands of Germans were to escape over the next week.

German commanders continued in their attempt to gain Hitler's support for a withdrawal. At Fifth Panzer headquarters, Dietrich sent a desperate warning to Army Group B that if the front held by the Fifth Panzer and Seventh Army was not withdrawn immediately and every effort made to move east out of the threatened encirclement, both would be lost. The enemy would be able to close in on the pocket from all sides. Von Kluge signaled Jodl, warning that such an encirclement should now be considered imminent.

In the drive toward Falaise, designated Operation TRACTABLE, the Canadians launched a massive armored thrust along the Orne to dislodge the Germans from their positions and seize the high ground north of Falaise. The operation

---

[6] Weigley, 207; Bradley, 377.

began shortly before noon on August 14, advancing behind a massive smoke screen that soon mingled with dust over the battlefield and served to reduce visibility for both sides. Following the example set by TOTALIZE, once again for TRACTABLE the offensive was preceded by an aerial bombardment, and again many Canadians and Poles fell victim to short-bombing—more than 150 killed and 241 wounded.[7] Incredulously, Bomber Command was using yellow target indicators, but the bombers had not been informed that yellow smoke was also the standard army recognition signal intended to alert friendly aircraft to the presence of Allied troops.[8] There were heavy casualties on both sides of the front line, but at the end of the day, the Germans were able to hold their ground and prevent a Canadian breakthrough.

Hitler later described the next day, August 15, as the worst day of his life.[9] All around him there was bad news closing in on all fronts. Allied forces began their landings on the French Mediterranean Coast under Operation ANVIL. The uprising in Warsaw by the Polish Home Army under General Bor-Komorowski was in its second week and was becoming more bitter and costly. To the east, the Russian steamroller now threatened the Ploesti oil fields of Rumania. In Normandy, German lines at Falaise were on the verge of collapse; I Panzer Corps was exhausted and the 85th Division almost wiped out. The British and Canadians were attacking LXXXVI Corps as it withdrew across the Dives River. Eberbach's troops at Alençon were on the defensive. To make matters worse, von Kluge had gone missing.[10]

Still suspicious of von Kluge's loyalty, Hitler feared that he was attempting to negotiate the surrender of the German Army of the West to the British and Americans.[11] Earlier that day, von Kluge had set out to meet with Hausser and ask for his support in securing Hitler's permission for a withdrawal, but

---

[7] Copp, 229; Stacey, 243.
[8] Copp, 229; Stacey, 243.
[9] Keegan, 255.
[10] OKW, 91.
[11] Weigley, 215.

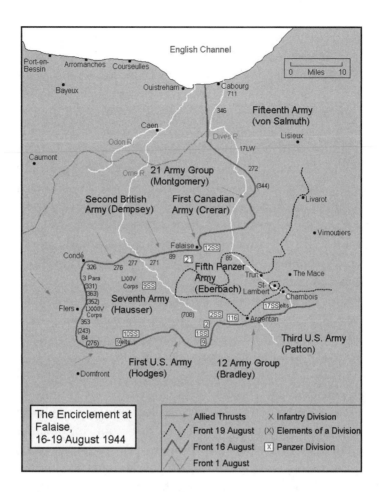

The Encirclement at Falaise, 16-19 August 1944

arriving too late for the meeting, he found that Hausser had already left. Taking his son with him, von Kluge set out after Hausser but came under attack by Allied aircraft. His car was put off the road and his communications truck destroyed. Out of contact with von Kluge, Blumentritt called OKW to report that his commander was missing. It is thought possible that von Kluge had intended to arrange a rendezvous with British and American negotiators, but had missed them owing to clogged roads and air attacks outside Falaise. By the time von Kluge returned to his headquarters, Hitler had already made plans to replace him with Field Marshal Walter Model, leaving orders for von Kluge to return to Berlin.

The Falaise pocket had shrunk to thirty-five miles in depth and only twelve miles wide at its opening. Hausser's Seventh Army and most of Eberbach's Fifth Panzer Army were still inside. The Canadians were at the outskirts of Falaise when Hitler signaled von Kluge that the town was to be held at all costs. Von Kluge stated flatly to his aides, "He's absolutely out of his mind." The Allies were taking hundreds of prisoners, with many POW groups—soldiers of the 1st SS Panzer, 89th Infantry, and 85th Infantry—reporting that their officers were desperately grabbing troops from anywhere they could be found and forming them up into ad hoc battle groups. The only remaining escape route through the Falaise Gap ran along the valley of the Dives River and through the opening between Trun and Chambois.

On August 16, Field Marshal von Kluge at last received permission to retreat to the east.[12] Although the withdrawal was to begin the next day, von Kluge contacted Hausser, Eberbach, and Dietrich immediately. By the next morning, the pocket had shrunk to an area of six by seven miles. Montgomery finally changed the U.S.-British boundary at Falaise, but it was too late to close the gap. Tens of thousands of exhausted Germans were still trying to escape. Six army or corps headquarters and twelve divisional headquarters moved northeast in convoys under steady artillery bombardment from a closing ring of Allied ground forces and fighter-bombers. Three thousand wrecked vehicles, abandoned guns, and wagons littered the roads, with the stench of dead soldiers and horses hanging thickly in the air.

Knowing that his recall to Berlin meant death, von Kluge wrote a letter expressing his faithfulness to Hitler and then took a cyanide pill. He had stood fifth on the army list as one of Germany's most senior officers. In disgrace, he had written on August 18: "I cannot bear the accusation that I sealed the fate of the West by taking wrong measures."[13] He then urged the Führer to end the war if the new weapons he was so eagerly

---

[12] Stacey, 254; Copp, 236; OKW, 92.
[13] Blumenson, 536.

awaiting did not bring success. "The German people have borne such untold suffering that it is time to put an end to this frightfulness." Always political, von Kluge closed with, "I depart from you, my Führer, as one who stood nearer to you than you perhaps realized, in the consciousness that I did my duty to the utmost."[14] Hitler read the suicide note the next day and handed it over to Jodl without any comment. He denied von Kluge any military honors at his funeral.

Field Marshal Model arrived at OB West headquarters on August 17 with orders from Hitler to assume command of the West Army. He was a master of defense, known as "Hitler's Fireman," the man upon whom the Führer relied in the most difficult situations. Before his arrival in Normandy, Model had been responsible for stabilizing the front of Army Group Center in the east. He enjoyed the complete trust of the Führer. Model met with Hausser, Dietrich, and Eberbach to be briefed on realities—morale, desertions, and Allied air attacks. He had arrived in Normandy believing that the situation could be managed by the right commander, but quickly realized that von Kluge had been correct: The Western Front was in a state of collapse. Model was loyal to Hitler, but he was also a realist. He issued a blunt assessment of the situation to OKW. When he suspected that his reports were being withheld from Hitler, he sent the original messages directly. No miracles would materialize under his command, however, and on August 18 Model ordered a full retreat east out from the pocket. What followed can only be described as a stampede through the Falaise Gap. Remnants of the 12th SS, 9th SS, and 2nd SS Panzer Divisions were ordered to hold the north shoulder of the pocket while the 2nd and 116th Panzers manned the southern wall of the corridor. The gap was now less than five miles wide. Trun formed the apex of the triangle, with Falaise and Argentan at the base.

The race to close the Falaise Gap came to an end on August 19 when Polish, Canadian, and British forces linked up with the U.S. 90th Infantry at Chambois. The line was thinly held and

---

[14] Stacey, 255.

Germans continued to pour through. General Hausser was badly wounded by shrapnel but escaped through the gap on the back of a tank. Eberbach replaced Hausser in command of the Seventh Army while Dietrich took over the Fifth Panzer Army for Eberbach. Rainy weather kept Allied aircraft on the ground during August 20–21, lending assistance to the German retreat. Upon visiting the Falaise area, Eisenhower wrote that "Roads, highways, and fields were so choked up with destroyed equipment and with dead men and animals, that passage through the area was extremely difficult. . . . [It was] literally possible to walk for hundreds of yards at a time, stepping on nothing but dead and decaying flesh."[15]

Tens of thousands of Germans were lost in the Falaise pocket, killed or wounded while trying to escape or taken prisoner. It is likely, however, that twenty to forty thousand others escaped through the gap between August 20 and 23, taking approximately one hundred tanks and artillery pieces with them.[16] The Allies had hoped to cut them off before they reached the Seine, but bad weather prevented supporting air attacks while eighteen ferries operated day and night to evacuate German forces across the river. From August 20 to 24, 300,000 soldiers and 25,000 vehicles of all types were ferried across to the east bank of the Seine,[17] and on the far shore, the German army began a period of reorganization as it prepared to meet the next Allied offensive. The Battle of Normandy was lost, and the remainder of France would soon follow, but the remnants of two German armies from the Falaise pocket were now streaming east towards the German border and the Siegfried Line, the massive defensive barrier known to the Germans as the West Wall. Here, they would once again confront the Allied advance in Northwest Europe.

✠

---

[15] Gilbert, 574.
[16] D'Este, 430–31, 456; Weigley, 214.
[17] Stacey, 294.

TO CHIEF OF OKW OPERATIONS STAFF, FOR INFORMATION OF C.-IN-C. WEST, AUGUST 10, 1944

The American forces have broken into the southern flank of the Army Group with 1 armored division, 3 motorized infantry divisions, and two smaller motorized cavalry detachments, and have now captured the area from Le Mans to the east. Now they have obviously turned across the line Mayenne–Beaumont–Bonnetable–La Ferte Bernard to the north.

It seems therefore that they are working in cooperation with the British who are expected to continue their push on Falaise, and thus close in on the 5th Panzer Army and the 7th Army from two sides. The use of fighter-bombers and bombers is significant, and they are dropping carpets of bombs in advance of the enemy spearheads in the Beaumont and Bonnetable areas.

The units of the 9th Armored Division which are at present fighting under G.H.Q. LXXXI Army Corps, and other scattered units are not able to offer protection for the south flank or to keep open the Alencon-Flers road, which is vital for bringing supplies.

It should therefore be considered whether a short and sharp tank attack would not destroy these enemy spearheads which are advancing northwards, and thus ensure the basis for the successful continuation of the battle, and pave the way for a decisive attack. However, these armored formations could only be transferred from the Mortain district for a short time, and would have to be under the command of General Eberbach for their task, which would be limited in duration, and restricted to a certain area.

The attack on Avranches could not take place until August 20, because of the weather, which is favorable for the enemy, and the length of time it would take to bring up the troops. Therefore this thrust to the south would not postpone any other operations. I request a decision.

(signed) von Kluge

✠

TELEPHONE CONVERSATION BETWEEN CHIEF OF GENERAL STAFF C.-IN-C. WEST AND CHIEF OF GENERAL STAFF OF ARMY GROUP, AUGUST 11, 1944

Chief of General Staff C.-in-C. West reports that according to a message from Chief of OKW Operations Staff about the situation report, dated August 10, which went through Army Group, the Führer requests immediate replies to the following questions:

(1) Why cannot the attack by the Eberbach Group start before August 20?

(2) What is your opinion of the attack from the present front of the XXXXVII Panzer Corps, thrusting in the old direction, bearing in mind the enemy's position?

(3) When, with what forces, and from which area could an attack towards Le Mans be made?

(4) When could the 11th Panzer Division with battle headquarters reach Tours, to attack Le Mans from there?

Field Marshal Walter Model became C-in-C West and commander of Army Group B after von Kluge's suicide. Known as "Hitler's fireman," Model was a master of flexible defense and enjoyed a close relationship with the Führer. In late September, he coordinated the German victory over Montgomery's MARKET GARDEN campaign.

(5) If the attack towards Avranches cannot be effected before August 20 then an attack on the XV American Corps must be started earlier.

As exact data are required for a decision of such importance, an answer should arrive tonight.

In reply to questions concerning conduct of attack:

To question (1)
Because according to Paragraph 3 of the Führer's order all formations to be freed cannot be ready until August 20.

The 331st Infantry Division which has arrived from the 15th Army cannot be used in the attack because it is vitally needed in the north (363rd Infantry division is almost totally annihilated).

The 85th Infantry Division in the area north of Falaise must remain where it is (89th Infantry Division has been more or less destroyed, and the 12th SS Panzer Division "Hitler Youth" suffered heavy losses in the last attack).

The other divisions which will also be sent into the attack cannot arrive at the attack assembly point at Domfront before August 20.

The battle group of the 6th Parachute Division (only 1 reinforced regiment) had to be sent to the area south of Alencon (forward units arrive early on August 11) because the situation there threatens to be dangerous. This is in accordance with the Führer's order Paragraph 6b.

To question (2)
I have just had a conference with General Eberbach, who was in the battle area until 24 hours ago, and he states that such an attack would not have much chance of success.

   Because:
   (a) The enemy on this front has been reinforced.
   (b) There would be no element of surprise.
   (c) Our battle strengths and the number of tanks would need to be considerably increased because with the troops and materials already there, no attack could be

made. They also need considerable supplies of fuel and artillery ammunition and this could not be done in a few days.

(d) In the face of enemy air superiority, we could only hope to launch a large-scale night attack. This could only be done if the weather were to change, and that cannot be expected in the immediate future. There is no moon, and that increases the difficulty of attacking and moving by night.

Our judgement of the fighting capacity of the troops does not coincide with that of General Hausser. I will find a solution to this vital question today after a personal discussion.

To question (3)

With the Panzer Division so weak in men and equipment, we would need to bring at least 2 of the best divisions from the Alencon area. The disposition of forces is dependent on the developments of the situation, which cannot yet be foreseen.

Advance during the night of August 11/12. They should break through on August 13, 14 and 15. (As far as possible the battle should be fought during the day, although even then the enemy air superiority is undisputed—see report on carpet bombing dated August 10). These are the most optimistic calculations, and are based on the assumption that the enemy have no more troops available apart from those already brought in.

Owing to the shortage of tanks, the Panther Detachment of the 9th Panzer Division would have to be used.

To question (4)

The 11th Panzer Division cannot be assembled in Tours before August 18 or 19, even if they start loading at 1400 hours on August 11.

(signed) von Kluge, Field Marshal

✠

TO CHIEF OF OKW OPERATIONS STAFF, FOR INFORMA-
TION OF C.-IN-C. WEST, RESULT OF CONVERSATION
WITH THE C.-IN-C. ON AUGUST 11, 1944

Yesterday evening SS General Hausser was of the opinion that
the attack in the direction of Avranches would be possible
after the forces had been regrouped.

His attitude today is as follows:

No longer practicable, as the enemy have brought in new
forces which could no longer be defeated by the ever dwin-
dling forces of the Panzer division, especially in view of the
numbers of enemy tanks, and the enemy mastery of the air.
The thrust to the sea could no longer be a rapid one, but
would be a prolonged and tough battle, and the panzer troops
are no longer equal to it.

Both the C.-in-C's are now of the same opinion.

I am in complete agreement with this decision, and wish to
add the following remarks: In a very short time the position on
the extreme southern wing of the Army Group has deterio-
rated, because of the deep enemy penetrations to the north,
and the strong enemy air support (bomber units). At the
moment the 9th Panzer Division is fighting near Alencon with
its back to the vital supply bases.

The putting in of the battle group of the 6th Parachute
Division (at present only a reinforced battalion, and the whole
only a reinforced regiment) which took place today is only a
negligible addition to our forces.

To improve the situation at this point panzer forces must
be brought in on this wing immediately, so that they can attack
the enemy under the command of General Eberbach.

During the night of August 11/12, the 116th Panzer Division could be released, and the 1st SS Panzer Division "Adolf
Hitler Bodyguard" and the 2nd Panzer Division released on
the night of August 13. These units can only be released however, if the outward salient in the 7th Army front line were
shortened towards the east. All of this means that for practical
purposes the idea of a push to the sea must be abandoned.

German prisoners of war captured during the drive to Falaise. After capturing Caen and Verrières Ridge in July, British and Canadian forces advanced south toward Falaise.

As the position on the extreme left wing of the Army deteriorates hourly, an over-all decision must be reached, and it must come as follows:

(a) Attack and defeat the enemy near Alencon with all available armored forces.

(b) Bring in more divisions on this wing, and so ensure the safety of the Army Group's wing by an attack to the west.

I request an immediate decision, so that the first unit can be withdrawn tonight.

von Kluge, Field Marshal

TO CHIEF OF OKW OPERATIONS STAFF, TELEPHONE CONVERSATIONS BETWEEN FIELD MARSHAL VON KLUGE AND GENERAL JODL, ON AUGUST 11, AT 1520 HOURS

(1) Withdrawal of the western outward salient of the 7th Army on the night of August 11/12 intended along line La Lande Vaumont-Vongeons-Soudeval-heights east of Mortain-south of Rancoudray.

(2) Assembly of attacking force in the Gandelain area–St. Cyr en Pail–Carrouges–La Motte Fouque.

(3) Composition of the attacking force:

Commander: General Eberbach with XXXXVII Panzer Corps and LXXXI Army Corps.

1st SS Panzer Division "Adolf Hitler Bodyguard"

2nd Panzer Division

116th Panzer Division

8th and 9th Mortar Brigades

1 heavy artillery detachment.

A fourth panzer division will probably be sent later.

(4) Start of the attack: Probably at dawn on August 14.

(5) Intended direction of the attack: From north-west to south-east, all 3 panzer divisions in a line.

Western panzer division from the area St. Cyr en Pail–Pre en Pail in the direction of Fresnay sur Sarthe.

Central panzer division from the area La Lacelle towards the crossroads at La Hugue.

Eastern panzer division from the Gandelain area toward Rouesse Fontaine. Direction of the thrust will be reviewed according to the situation.

von Kluge, Field Marshal

✠

The Führer has ordered:

"The serious threat to the deep southern flank of Army Group B renders it necessary to eliminate the danger by attacking.

(1) The American XV Army Corps in the area Le Mans–Mamers–Alencon is to be destroyed by a concentrated attack. To this end the attacking enemy forces are to be smashed deep in the flank by a strong formation of tanks coming from an approximate line Sille-Guillaume-Beaumont in the direction of Alencon and Mamers. When the 9th Panzer Division has thus been eased of its difficulties it is to join this attack from the north. General Eberbach will be in complete command.

(2) In order to release the Panzer Corps for this attack, forces inside the 7th Army sector are to be sent south. I am in complete agreement with a limited withdrawal of the front between Sourdeval and Mortain to release forces. The main point of the defense of the rest of the front must be centred on both flanks in the area around Falaise and Mortain.

(3) A group of infantry divisions is to be formed around Chartres (338th and 48th Infantry Divisions and later the 18th Luftwaffe Field Division) under the command of 1st Army H.Q., so that they will be able to protect Paris and the rear of Army Group B. They are to be sent from there forward to the Le Mans area as soon as possible, to mop up this area after the withdrawal of General Eberbach. Anti-tank troops with anti-tank guns and anti-tank close range weapons are to press along the important roads leading west to stop enemy armored cars and tank raiders approaching Paris. All the forces available in Paris are to be placed along the roads and block the way into the city from the west and south-west.

(4) You are to keep to the idea of attacking towards the sea to the west, taking Mayenne and the district to the north if necessary, after defeating American XV Army Corps.

A group of German soldiers captured by Canadians at St.-Lambert-sur-Dives is being marched into captivity on August 19, 1944. While 50,000 soldiers from Hausser's Seventh Army and Eberbach's Fifth Panzer Army were taken prisoner and another 10,000 killed, thousands were able to escape through the Falaise Gap before it was closed on August 21. In total disarray and without much of their equipment, the remnants of Army Group B withdrew toward Germany.

(5) For the time being the 11th Panzer Division will remain as rearguard support and the sole mobile reserve of the 19th Army.

(6) Plans to be reported in detail. Also report the intended grouping of all panzer and SS detachments in the Army Group."

Addendum by Army Group B:

Appendices will follow. Apart from the troops already ordered to be transferred by the 7th Army to General Eberbach, the 7th Army is also to send the Panther Detachment of the 9th Panzer Division to this group.

G.H.Q., Army Group B

✠

TO ARMY GROUP B, AUGUST 13, 1944

Estimate of the situation

Because of the new directive from the Führer the task will fall to the 7th Army of holding the assembly area for the thrust to the coast which is planned to take place later. Apart from this, the success of General Eberbach's Panzer Group in keeping the rear and flank free from enemy attacks is dependent on whether or not the 5th and 7th Armies can hold the front. If, as has been announced, more armored detachments have to be withdrawn this will have to be done by 4 battle-weary divisions.

In opposition to this thinly-manned front line the enemy have 8 infantry divisions and $3\frac{1}{2}$ armored divisions, which weaken the strength of our forces daily by continual attacks. Opposite the southern flank of the Army, which is only guarded by very weak forces, the enemy have another 3 infantry divisions, and when the Eberbach Panzer Group begin their thrust, we can expect these troops to become active. In these circumstances it seems to be necessary either to strengthen the 7th Army forces for their task, which is essential to the completion of the operation, by sending them infantry detachments and anti-tank weapons, or to give up the salient in the front line which juts out to the west, and by firmly holding the Falaise area, build up a north-south front line, which would make for a shorter front line and narrower sectors, and would strengthen the weak defenses south of Domfront.

With that in mind, the disadvantages of giving up valuable territory seems to be less. Until the mobile forces of the Panzer Group are strong enough to begin an operative thrust towards the sea, after they have cleared up the position deep in the Army Group flank, it seems to be more important to have a fortified front line through Falaise, Flers and Domfront or south of it so as to have a good base, than to have to run a continual risk of having the present front line broken up and a new enemy thrust near Domfront and to the south of it.

G.O.C. 7th Army

✠

TO CHIEF OF OKW OPERATIONS STAFF FOR THE INFORMATION OF C.-IN-C. WEST AND LUFTFLOTTE 3, AUGUST 13, 1944

The British forces, with 7 infantry divisions, 2 armored divisions and 3 armored brigades are at the moment east of the Orne ready to begin an attack towards Falaise and the southeast; British and American forces, with 15 infantry divisions, 4 armored divisions and 7 armored brigades, are on the north and west fronts of the 5th Panzer Army and the 7th Army. 3 motorized divisions and 1 armored division could attack the loose defenses of the southern front.

The American XV Army Corps with 2 infantry divisions and 2 armored divisions, had thrust between Alencon and Mortagne towards the north; but on August 12 they turned west, being covered from the north, to attack the 7th Army in the rear, or to meet the expected attack by our panzer forces. Further enemy forces (units of the American XX Army Corps) seem to have been brought up.

It seems therefore that the enemy are trying by all possible means to surround the bulk of the 5th Panzer Army and the 7th Army. To counter this, units of the 116th Panzer Division belonging to the Eberbach Panzer Group (battle H.Q. at Vieux Pont) had to engage such a superior foe at Sees on August 12 that although they were able to hold the enemy temporarily they could not stop his wheeling to the west. This division was pushed to the north during the course of the costly battle, and is now stationed on both sides of Argentan to prevent further enemy advances.

The 1st SS Panzer Division "Adolf Hitler Bodyguard" in their eastward march only reached the road on both sides of Ranes at 1100 hours on August 13. They had been held up by waves of fighter-bombers attacking them. Like the 2nd Panzer Division which is following them up, they will probably enter the fighting by a west-east movement, to safeguard the rear. With the present panzer divisions so weakened, it will be necessary, if we hope for unqualified success, to bring as quickly as possible more panzer detachments—9th and 10th SS Panzer

General of Panzer Troops Heinrich Eberbach took command of the Seventh Army after General Paul Hausser was injured at Falaise on August 19. Eberbach was then captured by British troops during the withdrawal across the Seine.

Divisions, 21st Panzer Division—especially as their assembly area is being constantly diminished by the enemy penetrations.

The situation therefore requires that we clear the enemy from the rear of our armies. That will mean attacking the American XV Army Corps, even while our supplies, in particular munitions and fuel, are being constantly depleted.

I therefore suggest, in complete agreement with all the higher commanders at the Army Group, that we retire to a line centred on Flers during the night of August 14/15, thus freeing our armored forces from the battle, and then we could transfer all our armored forces to the Eberbach Group so that they could be used for an offensive, with the exception of the battle group of the 2nd SS Panzer Division, which would have to take over the defense of the southern flank.

If the widely spread front line remains as it is at present, with its critical lack of resources, it will be broken through and surrounded by the enemy, with his superiority in men and materials, and his mastery of the air, and our units could not fight their way out.

Further measures will be decided during the course of events. I request instructions for the conduct of the battle in the sector of C.-in-C. West.

von Kluge

✠

WEEKLY REPORT, AUGUST 8–14, 1944

Estimate of the situation

At the moment the enemy have roughly 50 divisions in France, and also strong G.H.Q. troops. 31 divisions are still in Great Britain, and further forces are standing ready in America. The transport across the Channel continues at an increased rate.

As the main objective in their attempt to force a break-through on the front the enemy are trying to close in from two sides on the bulk of the 5th Panzer Army and the 7th Army and thus surround them. The southern arm of this pincers move-ment (American XV Army Corps with possibly also the Ameri-can XX Army Corps following them up) have crossed the Mortagne-Alencon line, and under cover from the east and north have swung west, so that they can strike at the 7th Army from the rear, and catch up with our Panzer forces which are coming up. In cooperation with that we can expect an enemy attack to start east of the Orne.

The enemy would not begin new operations until they have settled the battle with the 5th Panzer Army and the 7th Army. The fact that they are only feeling their way east from the Le Mans area with reconnaissance units also points to this conclusion. American units reinforced by French Resistance groups are continuing the battle for the fortresses in Brittany.

The High Command of the Allied invasion troops under General Eisenhower has been moved, and this is further proof that they do not intend any further large-scale landings on the west coast of Europe by sea. However, we can expect a large-scale landing in greater force by the airborne troops being prepared in Britain, to share in the operations against the Army Group.

Army Group B will assemble the bulk of the panzer detachments in the south-eastern flank under the command of General Eberbach, so that they can destroy the enemy in the Alencon area.

The question of supplying the fighting front in all areas has become more difficult as a result of the increase in air activity. The lack of mobility is becoming increasingly awkward.

Since June 6, our army and SS units have destroyed:

3,370	enemy tanks
475	aircraft

Our losses for the period June 6 to August 13, 1944 were:

3,630	officers (including 14 generals, 10 general staff officers, 243 C.Os.)
151,487	NCO's and men
3,813	Russians

158,930 men

We have received as replacements:

> 30,069 men.
> 9,933 men are on the way.

For the Army Group High Command,

The Chief of General Staff,
Speidel

WEEKLY REPORT, AUGUST 15–21, 1944

Estimate of the situation

The enemy now has in France about 53 divisions and strong G.H.Q. troops, which are combined in the British 21st and the American 12th Army Groups under General Eisenhower. There are 30 more divisions in Britain ready to come over to the mainland of Europe and further reinforcements can be expected from the U.S.A.

After the end of the battle with the 7th Army and after essential units have broken free, the enemy are trying to surround the forces south of the Seine downstream from Paris. The American XV Army Corps with 3 motorized divisions and 1 armored division crossed the Nollencourt-Houdan line in a northward direction on August 18, and have reached the Seine at a point between Vernon and Mantes; spearheads have already crossed the river. It seems that they are trying with the bulk of their forces to press to the north-west from south of the Seine and cut off the 5th Panzer Army and the remains of the 7th Army from their rear communications. Thus the enemy are showing their obvious intention of finishing off our forces in the Normandy area and then turning eastwards.

Simultaneously with this, 2 corps are operating between Chartres and the Loire, with the intention of bypassing Paris to the south, proceeding east and capturing the Loing and Seine crossings. According to previous experiences, we should be able to expect them to turn in towards Paris from the south-east. The enemy have only sent reconnaissance units against the ring of defenses around Paris.

In conjunction with these operational intentions, there is always the possibility of a large-scale landing by the airborne troops standing ready in Britain, although only weak airborne forces are being used in southern France. American units are striving to overcome the heroic resistance of the garrison at St. Malo and the fortresses of Brest, Lorient and St. Nazaire. The French Resistance groups are becoming more and more active.

Army Group B is striving to wipe out the enemy forces which are attempting a pincers movement south of the Seine, and to assemble the bulk of the panzer detachments on the eastern flank under General Eberbach.

Enemy air activity rose to immense proportions this week, and in many cases rendered it impossible for us to move our troops. For a brief period supplies could only be brought to the troops with fighter escorts. Our inferior mobility is hampering our tactical decisions.

Army and SS units have destroyed since June 6 3,663 tanks and 494 aircraft.

Our own losses have not yet been assessed.

For the Army Group High Command,

The Chief of General Staff,
Speidel

CHAPTER 6

Withdrawal across the Seine and the Miracle in the West, August 22–October 11, 1944

After the German withdrawal from Normandy, Hitler held firm in his decision to defend Paris to the last, ignoring the fact that there were no longer sufficient forces in the region to carry out his orders. On the morning of August 25, American forces entered Paris, led by a Free French contingent under General Leclerc. The German garrison offered some light resistance, but by 2:30 P.M., General von Choltitz surrendered the city. The liberation of the former French capital was of greater symbolic than strategic value, yet when von Choltitz disregarded the Führer's order to leave Paris in ruins Hitler viewed the surrender as an act of betrayal. Outside Paris, and throughout northern France, German forces were conducting a massive withdrawal to the east in an attempt to escape across the Seine. The German Army of the West did not pause in its retreat until it reached more defensible positions on the great northern European waterways, the Scheldt, the Meuse, and the tributaries of the Rhine.

The collapse of their defenses in Normandy led the Germans to abandon most of France. Over the past few weeks, the survival of Army Group B had depended more upon decisions made by local commanders than upon any large-scale movements ordered by OKW. German troops were now retreating in disarray. Along the Seine, their forces were not strong enough to offer serious resistance, while at the same time, the German Nineteenth Army was in flight up the Rhone Valley as the south of France was evacuated in the face of the Allied ANVIL landings. The loss of France was a serious blow to OKW. Under German occupation, the country had supplied a major portion of the food, iron ore, bauxite, coal, and labor that was essential to the Nazi war effort. The Germans were also forced to leave some fifteen hundred tanks behind in France[1] and lost the use of the Atlantic ports along the Bay of Biscay, thus further restricting U-boat capabilities.

By the end of August, the Battle of Normandy was over. In eighty-eight days of fighting, the West Army had lost four hundred thousand soldiers as casualties or prisoners of war, while Allied losses amounted to slightly over two hundred thousand. Five panzer divisions had been destroyed and six severely mauled.[2] Twenty German infantry divisions were consumed in the fighting, with a further twelve suffering crippling losses. At the close of the campaign, three divisions were trapped in Brittany, and another left isolated in the Channel Islands. German equipment losses were also extremely high after their disordered retreat through the Falaise Gap: 20,000 vehicles, 500 assault guns, 5,500 field guns, and 3,545 aircraft had to be abandoned. During the Battle of Normandy, the West Army had fifty infantry and twelve panzer divisions in the field. Now only about twenty infantry and six panzer divisions retained any semblance of organization.[3] In real numbers, the situation was even worse as several panzer divisions had been reduced to about ten tanks each. Several infantry divisions were at one-quarter strength. In terms of combat effectiveness, the Allies had about twice as many infantry and armored divisions at their disposal as the fighting moved west of the Seine. The ratio for their tanks was about twenty to one, while their advantage in air-power was even more dramatic. The Allies had fourteen thousand combat and hundreds of reconnaissance aircraft, while the Luftwaffe's Third Air Fleet had been reduced to 573 planes of all types.

Allied optimism that the war would soon be at an end seemed justified as August came to a close. About five Allied divi-

---

[1] D'Este, 456, 518; Weigley, 31.
[2] D'Este, 517–18.
[3] D'Este, 431; Stacey, 319.

sions were pressing on the general area of Elbeuf on the Seine, while to the east, Canadian and British troops later advanced toward Calais and Brussels. Hitler's faith that his advanced weaponry would turn the tide of the war remained unrealized: the British defenses were finally getting the better of the V-1 flying bomb. Of the ninety-seven sent out on August 28, twenty-three were shot down by British aircraft and sixty-five by anti-aircraft guns.[4] Five V-1s reached the outskirts of London while another four fell on the city itself. By the end of the month, the Allied bombing campaign against German synthetic fuel plants and oil fields in southeastern Europe intensified, with sixty bombing raids taking place since August 7. On the eastern front, the Red Army had reached the border of East Prussia and the Rumanian oil fields at Ploesti were in Russian hands. Soviet troops were now within three hundred miles of Berlin.

Allied troops, over Montgomery's objections, were now divided into two army groups.[5] The 21st Army Group, composed of British and Canadians under Montgomery, was assigned to the northeast Pas de Calais region while the American 12th Army Group, under Bradley, cleared Brittany and built up strength for an advance eastward from Paris towards Metz. Both army groups fell under Eisenhower's personal control when he assumed command of Allied ground forces on September 1. Montgomery believed there should be one single powerful thrust towards Germany and that dividing the armies would weaken them, with neither having sufficient strength to push through to Germany.[6] Others, however, envisioned the remainder of the campaign in northwest Europe as a victorious advance on a broad front, and nearly everyone except Churchill thought the war would be over by Christmas. It was soon discovered that the Allies had underestimated the German Army's capacity for recovery and resistance.[7]

In northern France, Allied forces consisted of four armies. To the north, on the left flank, was the Canadian First Army.

---

[4] Gilbert, 582.
[5] Stacey, 308.
[6] Stacey, 309–10, 316–19.
[7] Blumenson, 687–88, 702.

The center group consisted of the British Second Army and
U.S. First Army. To the south, on the right flank, was the U.S.
Third Army. In view of difficult supply problems hindering the
delivery of food, fuel, and ammunition to the forces, Eisenhower on August 24 ordered the U.S. First and Third Armies to
halt their advance in order to support Montgomery's operations in the northeast.[8] Logistical problems were growing more
serious as the armies advanced, exacerbated by the far greater
consumption of supplies by Allied divisions compared to the
Germans: seven hundred tons a day as opposed to two hundred. Meanwhile, the German hold over the English Channel
ports rendered Allied forces dependent upon truck deliveries
from Normandy in order to sustain their advance.

The Allies had pushed out a great salient from Abbéville in
the north and Orléans in the south, with the apex at Verdun.
Supply problems, however, prevented them from mounting an
effective pursuit on all four army fronts. Recognizing his
enemy's difficult supply situation, Hitler placed a priority on
holding the ports of Le Havre, Boulogne, Dunkirk, and Calais.
The Allies were already supplying the U.S. Third Army by air-
lift and now faced the hard decision of which armies would be
brought to a halt in order to accumulate sufficient fuel to sustain the others in their pursuit. Tensions soon rose among the
Allied leaders, who were faced with the impossibility of fully
exploiting their Normandy victory.

In the Allied center, the advance continued with a string of
individual victories bringing gradual progress toward Germany. To the west, the British Second Army made a remarkable advance of 110 miles in two days, liberating Brussels on
September 3. For three days and nights, Belgium celebrated
without restraint. The northern group of armies received
orders to seize the Pas de Calais ports and V-1 launching sites,
establish airfields in Belgium, and secure the harbor facilities
at Antwerp, the only port with both the capacity and location
to ease the Allied supply problem.

---

[8] Bradley, 400; Stacey, 308.

On September 4, the British made a sixty-mile dash from Brussels to capture the great inland port at Antwerp. The German garrison abandoned the city and there was no major battle. The Belgian resistance was able to help prevent serious damage to the port. These facilities would not be useable, however, until both banks of the fifty-mile Scheldt estuary leading out to the English Channel were in Allied hands. Von Zangen's Fifteenth Army was still strong numerically but seriously impeded by lack of fighting experience. They were surrounded, but as long as they held the banks of the Scheldt, there would be no solution to the Allied supply problem.[9]

On September 5, Field Marshal von Rundstedt arrived at the newly-established headquarters in Koblenz to resume his old position as C-in-C West. He replaced Field Marshal Model, who retained command of Army Group B after having found the administration of both headquarters extremely challenging.[10] As C-in-C of Army Group B, Model now had about twenty-five divisions with which to defend a front of four hundred miles. In the previous July, sixty-two German divisions had been hard-pressed to hold a front approximately one-quarter that length in Normandy. To make matters more difficult, Hitler was now calling on Army Group B to go on the offensive in Belgium and Holland.[11] With von Rundstedt back as C-in-C West, however, Model was, at least, spared the work of a massive combined headquarters.

Hitler sent Model orders for von Zangen to move the Fifteenth Army across the Scheldt in order to defend the Albert Canal line just north of Antwerp. The Channel fortresses guarding the approaches to the port city, Hitler declared, were to be "held preservingly."[12] Every day the Germans could maintain their grip on Antwerp and other Channel ports, the better their chances of building a strong defense along the Rhine and the line of fortifications known as the West Wall. To this

---

[9] Stacey, 320; Bradley, 401–5, 418–26.

[10] Ziemke, "Rundstedt," in Barnett, 201; OKW, 125.

[11] Stacey, 302.

[12] OKW, 130.

end, von Zangen was to create two new "fortresses"—Scheldt North and Scheldt South—in order to deny the Allies the use of Antwerp and its deep-water port.

While the Germans were preparing their defenses,[13] Eisenhower flew to see Montgomery in Brussels in order to settle the dispute over Allied strategy. He came away from the meeting having agreed to Montgomery's ambitious plan for extensive airborne landings, with Arnhem as the immediate objective. Montgomery was worried about obtaining sufficient supplies to launch the massive undertaking, but Eisenhower agreed to rein in Bradley's American armies in the southeast in order to provide logistical support for the new offensive, code-named Operation MARKET GARDEN. The plan called for three airborne divisions to be dropped simultaneously astride the road to Arnhem while supporting ground forces moved northward through Eindhoven and Nijmegen. Once bridges over the six major water obstacles had been seized, the way would be open for a turn east into Germany. Allied planners were buoyed by news that U.S. Army patrols had crossed the German border on September 11, while on the next day, I British Corps eliminated the last pocket of resistance at Le Havre. The Allies now held Belgium, Luxembourg, and part of Holland. To the south, the U.S. Army completed its advance up the Rhone Valley and made contact with French forces at Dijon on September 12. Despite the rapid American advance, most of von Blaskowitz's First and Nineteenth Armies from southern France managed to slip through to the east.

While preparations were underway for British and American troops to land at Arnhem, on September 13, Montgomery assigned the First Canadian Army the task of clearing the Scheldt. With all available resources being siphoned off for Operation MARKET GARDEN, however, Montgomery underestimated the task of opening up the approaches to Antwerp, where the Germans were determined to defend the mouth of the Scheldt.

---

[13] OKW, 156–59.

The German Army at this time was also mounting a concerted effort to restore the West Wall's system of blockhouses and bunkers. With its foundations laid down in 1936 and expanded in 1938–39 along the prewar Franco-German boundary, the wall had fallen into disuse after the defeat of France. Reactivating the fortifications was an enormous task. Everything moveable had been carted away for construction of the Atlantic Wall and many local farmers in recent years had taken to using the pillboxes as storehouses. Some of the firing slits designed for weapons in 1939 were too small for those used in 1944. There were not enough troops to garrison every strongpoint. There was also a shortage of divisions available to man the defenses; the 2nd SS "Das Reich" Panzer Division, for instance, took up positions along the wall covering a front of ten miles rather than the usual three miles. On September 15, the U.S. V Corps attacked the West Wall.[14] That same day, Hitler declared this line of fortifications to be of such decisive importance to the battle for Germany that every strongpoint was to be held to the last man's last round of ammunition.

Montgomery's Operation MARKET GARDEN began on September 17 with an armada of Allied aircraft passing over the front lines on their way to the drop zones. The seizure of the Eindhoven and Nijmegen bridges, the MARKET phase of the operation, was completed successfully, but GARDEN, the descent of the British 1st Airborne Division, went disastrously astray.[15] In their long march toward the Arnhem bridges, the paratroopers were surprised to find the area held by the remnants of the 9th SS and 10th SS Panzer Divisions, which were in the process of reorganizing after escaping the Falaise pocket. Between them, the two panzer divisions could muster only a company of tanks, along with some armored cars and half-tracks, but it was enough firepower to stop the lightly-armed British airborne who waited in vain for their armored support to arrive from the south. The Guards Armoured Division, advancing to join them, found itself bogged down by con-

---

[14] Weigley, 304.
[15] Stacey, 313.

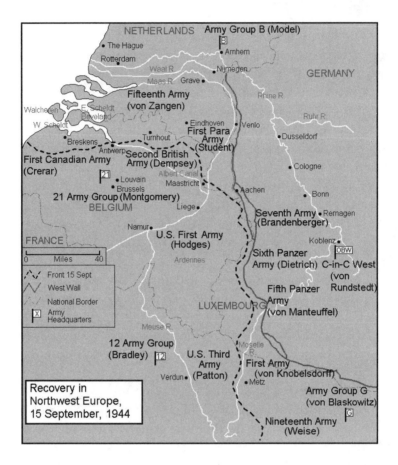

Recovery in
Northwest Europe,
15 September, 1944

gestion along a single road between flooded fields. The bold
Allied stroke to open the way into Germany had failed.

The German high command made no major strategic
adjustments as a result of MARKET GARDEN.[16] OKW still held the
continued defense of the Scheldt estuary to be of greater
importance than "cutting off the Arnhem finger." Heavy fighting broke out in the Dutch polders as Canadian troops made
an advance north from the Albert Canal, establishing a bridgehead at Turnhout Canal. Allied tactical airpower harassed von
Zangen's army, but there were few losses as many aircraft were
required to support other operations along the Channel coast
as well.

---

[16] OKW, 184.

Until September 23, the Germans believed that the purpose of MARKET GARDEN was to capture the Rhine bridges in order to outflank their forces *west* of the Eindhoven-Antwerp axis. They assumed that the Allies would have made Antwerp their priority. Unknown to them, Montgomery had decided that "Antwerp would have to wait." It was a very costly choice. The Scheldt estuary became the worst kind of battlefield imaginable as the understrength Canadian First Army slogged through flooded fields that lay below sea level. Knowing the importance of the ground they held, the Germans fought here with even greater resolution than usual.

With Operation MARKET GARDEN ending in disaster, the British received orders to withdraw from Arnhem on September 25.[17] Of 10,300 British paratroops who jumped at Arnhem, 7,500 became casualties. One thousand were killed in battle, five hundred wounded, and another six thousand taken prisoner. Arnhem was Germany's first major success since the withdrawal from Normandy. During this same period, the Germans also fought a highly successful defense at Aachen and reinforced their positions along the Scheldt estuary. With a surge of confidence, Hitler further ordered the destruction of the enemy in the Arnhem-Nijmegen area. In Germany, he ordered the conscription of all men from the ages sixteen to sixty to form a "People's Army," or home guard, to be equipped mostly with captured small arms.[18]

In the battle for the Channel ports the Canadians attacked the western defenses at Calais with heavy bomber support on September 25–26, finally taking it by the end of the month. Even with Calais, Le Havre, and Boulogne, however, the Allies needed to shorten their supply lines by seizing a port closer to the front. On October 13, Eisenhower ordered Montgomery to give priority to taking Antwerp before a drive for Germany's industrial heartland in the Ruhr could be considered.[19] The battle for the Scheldt had begun on October 4, but it would be

---

[17] Stacey, 316; Bradley, 418.

[18] Weigley, 256.

[19] Stacey, 389.

another two months before the first Allied convoy could enter Europe by way of Antwerp.

Pleading for reinforcements to enable him to defend the approaches to Antwerp, von Zangen received only verbal encouragement from von Rundstedt, who replied that reinforcements were simply not available, even though the Fifteenth Army's stand outside the port was of vital importance. "The attempt of the enemy to occupy the West Scheldt in order to obtain the free use of the harbor of Antwerp must be resisted *to the utmost.*" Model sent in the 85th Infantry Division "Battle Group Chill," his fire brigade from the Fifteenth Army tactical reserve, to reinforce the 70th and 346th Infantry in holding a firm line of defense.

At the beginning of September, Allied intelligence reports had assumed that the German Army was all but finished.[20] Instead, by the end of the month, the Germans had consolidated their lines, holding the Allies back along four fronts. Both the Allied advance toward the Ruhr and the quest for the Channel ports were bogging down. The U.S. First and Third Armies had each encountered severe resistance by German defenders and were forced to bring their advance to a halt. The British Second Army was unable to breach the West Wall fortifications and suffered a disastrous defeat at Arnhem. The Canadian First Army fought a bitter war of attrition along the Channel coast. With the "miracle in the West," the German command had succeeded in establishing a continuous line running from Breskens and Walcheren on the extreme right, northeast to Arnhem, and south toward Switzerland. Its forces were determined and well-entrenched. Many months of slow, bitter fighting lay ahead.

At this point, Hitler excitedly called his operations staff together to announce his next offensive on the western front— in the Ardennes. Von Rundstedt and Model's forces were now to receive priority in the allocation of equipment, food, and ammunition. Hitler guaranteed every man and tank would be at their disposal. With the element of surprise, impeccable

---

[20] Hinsley, 367–69.

planning, and his new V-2 rockets and jet aircraft, the Führer's forces would cut off the Allied armies, encircle, and destroy them. They would then seize Antwerp and stabilize the western front. This would allow Germany to once again turn its attention to the east and strike out against the Soviets. That, at least, was the state of the Führer's plans for continuing the war after October 1944.

✠

TO THE CHIEF OF THE COMBINED SERVICES HIGH COMMAND, GENERAL JODL, TO BE SUBMITTED TO THE FÜHRER, AUGUST 24, 1944

On the basis of the latest developments in the situation I have arrived at the following estimates of the strengths in the West:

I

The enemy now have about 53 divisions in north-west France, and could raise this number to 55 or 57 by September 1. There are about 8 divisions operating in southern France. All the enemy divisions are extensively motorized and mechanized.

In support of the ground operations they have about 7,000 fighters and 7,200 bombers in north-west France, and in southern France roughly 1,300 fighters and 900 bombers. (At any given time, from a third to a half of these are serviceable.)

The following possibilities are open to the enemy:

(a) After gaining the Seine bank crossings they could push northwards past Paris between Rouen and Mantes to the Somme. Their objectives would be the V-1 bases and the vital Belgian industrial basin. They could use 30–35 divisions for this thrust.

(b) Thrust through Paris towards Rheims to the traditional invasion route to Germany. They could use 35 divisions for this.

(c) West-east push south of Paris across the line Troyes-Auxerre in the direction of Dijon, so as to cut off Army

Group G, and then through the Belfort basin for a thrust to Alsace. 25 divisions could be used for this.

For all three operations they could use their airborne army to open up the way (Seine or Somme crossings).

They could conduct operations (a) and (b) simultaneously with 15 and 25 divisions respectively.

II

As was reported on August 18, our own troops are exhausted. We cannot expect appreciable reinforcements before September 1, and the promised replacements still later.

Work on the Somme-Marne positions has only been going on for a short time, and they are not yet ready for any defensive action. It is therefore essential to bridge the gap until at least September 1, because, if things go very badly, the enemy spearheads will in that time have reached the Somme positions, in the area east of Paris, or the Dijon area.

First of all the Seine position downstream from Paris is being manned: 4 H.Q. staffs have been put in there, the LXXXVI, LXXIV, LXXXI, XXXXVII Panzer Corps, with 12 divisions or divisional battle groups (711th, 346th, 3rd Paratroop, 353rd, 271st, 331st, 344th, 17th Luftwaffe Field, 49th, 18th Luftwaffe Field, 6th Paratroop and 275th).

One group from the panzer divisions (what is left of about 6 divisions, which are to be quickly renewed) must be placed under the H.Q.s of I and II SS Panzer Corps between the Somme and the Seine as mobile reserves, and at the same time be renewed. The bridgehead south of the Seine must be held as long as possible to make our crossings easier, and to keep the enemy forces in check. It will only be withdrawn when the advantages in holding it are outweighed by the disadvantages.

The problem of Paris is still urgent. Admittedly the 47th Division will be brought in there from August 25/26 to strengthen the defenses, but in the face of enemy pressure from the outside and with the increased danger inside the city, this reinforcement will not be sufficient for safety. We have

One of the three large coastal guns, of about 16-inch caliber, found intact at Le Trésorerie on September 19, 1944. Pursuing the Germans after their escape across the Seine, the British Second Army advanced toward Brussels, the First Canadian Army toward the Channel ports of the Atlantic coast, and the U.S. First and Third Armies toward southwest Germany.

therefore ordered a strong line to be set up just to the north and east of Paris.

We can only expect 3 infantry divisions (338th, 716th and 198th) to be sent back from Army Group G, with 1 panzer division, the 11th. The intention is to form from the panzer divisions a group (about 7 or 8 divisions) in the southern flank of the 1st Army, so that they can attack the enemy spearheads and thus cover the western flank of the 19th Army. 15 extra divisions will be necessary in addition to the forces already available, to hold the Seine-Yonne-Dijon line, and they will have to be assembled in the area Troyes–Dijon–Geneva Lake by September 10.

The 3 divisions from the north and the 15th Army area, which will be released by the arrival of the 36th, 553rd and

563rd divisions, will be urgently needed to build up a front on the right flank of the 1st Army. It is taken for granted that there will be sufficient Luftwaffe forces, roughly in the strength of at least 300 fighters ready to take off at any moment.

III

We will need for the Somme-Marne line altogether 4 Army H.Qs, 12 Corps H.Qs and at least 30 to 35 divisions at the front, 1 panzer army with 4 panzer H.Q. staffs, and 12 panzer divisions in reserve to counterbalance the enemy motor mechanized units.

If the enemy begin a strong campaign and bring in new forces, the possibility will have to be reckoned with that the Seine-Yonne-Dijon line cannot be held for long, and we may have to withdraw to the Somme-Marne line. Speedy construction work is therefore needed at the latter line, and a defense force, which can continue this work, is essential. For this we could use the very weak remains of the 12 divisions which need a rest (Remains of the 352nd, 84th, 89th, 326th, 363rd, 276th, 277th, 708th, 272nd, 273rd, 343rd and the 5th Paratroop Division).

Furthermore, the same must be done as on the eastern front. We must look ahead, and build more rearward positions behind the Somme-Marne line, extended to include the Western Wall.

I request the required instructions giving consent for this.

Model, Field Marshal

✠

TO CHIEF OF OKW OPERATIONS STAFF, TO BE PRESENTED TO THE FÜHRER, AUGUST 29, 1944

I report the following as supplement to the measures taken by Army Group B on August 28 and 29, 1944.

(1) Enemy position: The British Army Group (25–27 divisions) has begun a rapid thrust across the Seine to the north, concentrated on the eastern flank, with the intention of pressing our troops back to the sea, provided the breakthrough is successful, and capturing the V-1 bases. Apart from their heavy artillery and immense air superiority the enemy are able to put in up to 1,500 tanks between Paris and the coast. The American Army Group with the 12 divisions (including up to 1,200 tanks) at present in the area north of Paris–Soissons–Chalons s.M.–Vitry le Francois will continue to attack in a general north-easterly direction. This assumption is based on information from a reliable source, stating that the V Corps have been ordered to attack the towns of Montcornet and Rethel; according to the same source the XII Corps is to take the heights east of Chalons s.M. The XX Corps, between the V and XII Corps, is attacking Rheims. For the remaining 10–12 divisions of the American Army Group (including about 750 tanks) there are the possibilities of following up either towards Rheims or to the east through Troyes.

(2) Position of our troops: The divisions which have arrived from Normandy across the Seine under immense difficulties and after the hardest fighting have only a few heavy arms, and in general they are only armed with carbines. The supply of necessary personnel and material replacements is, as has been reported in detail, completely inadequate. After 5 battle-weary infantry divisions have been sent back to the Reich, there remains, with replacements and reassembling of the remains of the 11 Normandy infantry divisions, enough to form about 4 units, but they will only have equipment if the demands made in the order dated August 27 are fulfilled.

From the 6 SS panzer divisions and 5 army panzer divisions we could only form 1 regimental group, which could be the 11th Regimental Group, and that could only be done if we received replacements of men and equipment.

The panzer divisions now have 5–10 tanks each. With regard to artillery, the infantry divisions only have single guns left, and the panzer divisions have a single battery each.

At the moment the troops are strongly influenced by the enemy's superiority, especially in aircraft and tanks, and by the fighting in isolated pockets. Measures are being taken. The low degree of manoeuvrability of the infantry divisions, caused by the fact that their mobility is only an emergency expedient (horses), has proved to be a distinct disadvantage in the unequal struggle against a highly mobile enemy, especially as there is absolutely no reserve of assault guns and other heavy anti-tank guns. And so the units available and those which have been brought in from the coast are at the moment tactically inferior. A speedy alteration in these circumstances is the first consideration for successful operations.

With regard to the situation in the air, I wish to refer to my teleprinter message dated August 29, concerning the maintenance of the fighting capacity of the fighter units, which is of vital concern to the Army Group.

(3) The concentration of all available fast-moving units in the area Chalons-Rheims-Soissons, ordered by me on the evening of August 28, and reported at once to General Jodl by Chief of the General Staff of C.-in-C. West, was essential to ward off the swift and dangerous thrust carried out by the American Army Group against the rear of the 15th, 7th and 5th Panzer Armies. Considering the enemy position (see (1)), this meant that the right flank was in danger of an enemy tank attack, and on the left flank there was the possibility of a further enemy advance in the direction of Dijon.

The following temporary expedients are possible:

Withdrawing on the right flank to the Somme if necessary-this was requested by General Dietrich because of the condition of our troops, but I refused this until now.

Diverting to the left flank the reinforcements meant for the right flank of the 1st Army (559th Division and the 106th Panzer Brigade).

Only when the 347th and 553rd Divisions have been brought in, as I ordered, will it be possible to withdraw the fast-moving units in the area Soissons-Rheims-Chalons, which are supposed to come under the command of the 5th Panzer Army as from August 31. Otherwise there would be a dangerous gap left, which would speedily have dangerous consequences. It should here be emphasized that the fighting capacity of the Bittrich and Schwerin groups is very small. We can only expect any improvement when we receive more tanks and artillery.

Model, Field Marshal

✠

TO THE CHIEF OF OKW OPERATIONS STAFF, WITH THE REQUEST THAT IT BE SUBMITTED IN THE ORIGINAL TO THE FÜHRER, SEPTEMBER 4, 1944

(1) Enemy position: The British army group is making a concentrated thrust to the north-east, towards the Scheldt estuary (Antwerp), with the double intentions of capturing the V-1 bases and cutting off the 15th Army. The units which are still spread out in depth are now closing up.

An American battle group from the 12th Army Group with about 6–8 divisions has joined in this thrust, and can bring in more forces. At least 2,500 tanks might be used altogether in this operation.

The bulk of the 3rd American Army has been closing up in the Verdun area for the last 3 days, and could start an attack against the Luxembourg-Metz line at any time.

French and Belgian Resistance are joining the battle to an ever increasing extent. The large-scale airborne landing which is expected will most probably be in the region of the West Wall.

Altogether the enemy have brought up till now 55 divisions and strong forces of H.Q. troops into the north France battle-grounds, and in addition they could bring 30 more divisions from Britain and the transfer of further forces from the U.S.A.

(2) Position of our own troops: Our own troops, which in the meanwhile had suffered very heavy losses, were no match

against the enemy's superior equipment and great mobility, especially on the northern flank. They were repeatedly over-taken and cut off, as closely-linked panzer units, assault guns and anti-tank weapons were lacking as much for open warfare as for a local concentrated attack to delay the enemy advance. Otherwise the situation described in my report dated August 29th has become even worse, as the troops are daily becoming more exhausted.

At the moment we only have the following which are really fit for action:

(a) with the 15th Army, which includes the area under C.-in-C. Netherlands, about 4 infantry divisions, not count-ing the fortress garrisons.

(b) with the 5th Panzer Army, 3 or 4 panzer divisions and $1\frac{1}{2}$ or 2 infantry divisions.

The position is more favorable in the 1st Army area, as there has been no enemy pressure there since August 29.

After receiving the 19th, 553rd and 559th Divisions and the 106th Panzer Brigade they now have a battle force of about 3 panzer and panzer grenadier divisions, as well as $4\frac{1}{2}$ infantry divisions.

(3) We do not yet know how the 15th Army's attempts to break through are progressing. It seems that only some units will be able to fight their way through. The line Albert Canal–Maas–western positions can still be considered as the line to be held by Army Group B. But it will need to be manned by 25 fresh infantry divisions and an adequate armored reserve of 5–6 panzer divisions.

As a result of the developments on the western flank, 2 panzer brigades (besides the 105th) and several infantry divi-sions must be sent there immediately.

At least 10 more divisions and 5 more panzer divisions will be needed later (until September 15). Otherwise the approach to north-western Germany will be open. It is already necessary to provide powerful skeleton forces as quickly as possible for the western positions and the West Wall; the 11 fortress battal-ions and the 6 machine gun battalions which were expected

One of the coastal guns of the Atlantic Wall near Boulogne, September 21, 1944. The chain-mail camouflage screen over the gun was used as an anti-shrapnel cover for the gun crew. The Channel ports were taken by the Allies as they advanced northward, with Dieppe falling on September 1, Le Havre on September 12, Dunkirk on the sixteenth, Boulogne on the twenty-second, and Calais and the V-1 sites on October 1.

between September 15 and 20 will arrive too late. They must man the western positions earlier. Otherwise it is suggested that anti-aircraft units from Germany could be brought in in sufficient numbers.

The mobile battle force which the Führer has commanded to be formed on the southern flank, according to paragraph 2 of the order dated September 3, could then be formed from the following units:

3rd Panzer Grenadier Division
15th Panzer Grenadier Division
17th SS Panzer Grenadier Division
9th Panzer Division
106th Panzer Brigade

Battle groups of the 11th and 21st Panzer Divisions and 3 other panzer brigades.

For this 3 panzer divisions could possibly be transferred from the east.

Model, Field Marshal

✠

TO C.-IN-C. ARMY GROUP B, SEPTEMBER 7, 1944

I request that the following estimate of the situation, which was formed after a conference with Fieldmarshal Model, and based on the latest reports, be submitted to the Führer:

(1) Enemy position: At the moment the Anglo-Americans have in Belgium and northern France about 54 extensively motorized and mechanized divisions and very strong H.Q. forces. French and Belgian Resistance groups are supporting them to an ever increasing degree. There are still at least 30 divisions in England, including 6 airborne divisions which are ready to be brought over to the mainland. The transport of forces direct from the U.S.A. has begun.

The British 21st Army Group has taken from its 25–27 divisions about 8 or 10 divisions with probably 600 tanks between Boulogne and Antwerp for an extensive, partly encircling, attack against the units of the 15th Army which are cut off from the east. A second battle group between Antwerp and Diest is being prepared. Theirs will be the task of forcing a crossing of the Albert Canal, and of pressing on to Rotterdam and Amsterdam.

6 to 8 more British divisions with probably 400 tanks are now closing in, probably from the rearward areas. They could be used to augment the forces intended for the thrust into Holland, or to help the troops against the 15th Army, according to the requirements of the situation.

The fortress of Le Havre is being attacked by 2 or 3 divisions with about 100 tanks. Contrary to what is the case with other fortresses being attacked, it is important for the enemy to take this harbour, which is the most useful in France, as quickly as possible.

The fortresses of Dunkirk, Calais and Boulogne will involve for some time a number of the other divisions of the British forces at present engaged against the 15th Army.

The American 12th Army Group with 15 to 18 divisions and about 1,000 tanks is between Hasselt and Toul attacking to the east on a broad front, with the object of pushing on to the Rhine. To the rear of its northern flank 3 or 4 units are apparently being brought up.

The following points of concentration for attacks seem to be indicated:

(a) The area between Hasselt and the heights running from the east of Namur to the south of the Maas.

(b) Charleville-Sedan area.

(c) The area on both sides of, and especially south of Metz.

The southern flank, which at the moment is rather bent back, will probably be brought into line to coincide with the enemy advance from southern France against the Burgundy Gate.

In Brittany there are about 5 American divisions tied down by the fighting for the fortresses and attempting to enclose them.

(2) Against this must be stated: Our own troops are all engaged in the fighting, are being heavily attacked and are partly exhausted. They have no artillery or armored weapons. No reserves worth considering are available. The enemy's numerical advantage in tanks is complete. At the moment Army Group B has about 100 tanks. The enemy air forces control the battle area and the communications deep in the rear of our lines. The enemy pressure towards Liege (Meuse Valley), which is obviously directed against Aachen and the Rhine-Westphalia industrial region, has become a serious threat.

It seems to me to be of vital importance to bring up at once the strong forces which have so often been requested—at least 5, and if possible 10 divisions with assault artillery detachments and sufficient anti-tank weapons and also a number of panzer divisions.

All the forces at our disposal (the weak 9th Panzer Division, 1 weak panzer assault detachment, 2 assault gun brigades, with assault guns on the way) have been sent by C.-in-C. West to the Aachen area.

The 12th Grenadier Division has not yet arrived. In agreement with Fieldmarshal Model I perceive here the acute danger which also threatened the rear of the West Wall. No operative enemy airborne landings have taken place as yet. They can take place as the situation demands, either behind the West Wall, or also form a bridgehead on the eastern bank of the Rhine. They will take place wherever the enemy thrust towards the Rhine is successful.

It is our task to play for time with the forces available so that the western positions and the West Wall can be prepared for defense by the H.Q. authorities who have been entrusted with the job, together with units of the armed forces and the Party. The forces which have been reported to me as being intended for the forming of the western positions, 135,000 men all told, seem to me to be totally inadequate. Even if one includes all the rear units of the forces under the C-in-C. West, many more workers will be required along a line of positions more than 500 kilometers long. We do not fail to recognize the difficulties (equipment, billeting, supplies, etc.) in the organization of these auxiliary forces and the indefatigable work of all the Party officials, and civilian departments.

However, the whole organization takes time!

According to the information from the commander of the western fortresses, General Kuntze, the building of the western positions will require 6 weeks. This time must therefore be gained by fighting.

If I am to command with any possibility of success, I again demand that all available tanks be sent up at once apart from the forces intended for the Aachen area to protect the Rhine-Westphalia industrial area, and regardless of the consequences, to complete the panzer units and assault gun brigades, also a special delivery of all anti-tank weapons which can be mustered, which can afford the troops some method of defense against the enemy tanks.

The Führer has ordered me, regardless of the local losses on the front, to carry out an advance deep into the American east flank, in a north-westerly direction, from the area around Epinal. If a stronger panzer group subordinated to the 5th Panzer Army, which itself has been put at the disposal of the C.-in-C. West for this attack (but is instructed to cooperate with Army Group G.), is to be used, I consider it essential that 10,000 cubic metres of fuel should be brought up immediately. Also it will be necessary to have all available forces of the Luftwaffe for this attack, even if it means leaving the other fronts exposed.

(signed) von Rundstedt, Field Marshal

✠

TO C.-IN-C. WEST, FIELD MARSHAL VON RUNDSTEDT, SEPTEMBER 8, 1944

The situation of the 7th Army has developed in the last two days in a particularly threatening manner. The remains of this army which are still available will be able to offer temporary resistance in the Maas sector between Maastricht and Liege. South of Liege, as far as the newly announced Army Group boundary there is only a very thin and totally inadequate line of defenses. The enemy here enjoys practical freedom of movement as far as the West Wall, 120 km. length of which, behind the 7th Army, is manned by only 7 or 8 battalions.

Of the reinforcements which have already been reported, the 9th Panzer Division, which was detailed by C.-in-C. West on the evening of the 6th September, has not yet arrived, and the furthest forward division, the 12th Grenadier Division, is not expected to arrive until September 12. In any case, neither of these formations will be sufficient to carry out the present task allotted to them—the battle to gain time before the West Wall, followed by the holding of the West Wall itself.

If 3 infantry divisions and 1 panzer division cannot be transferred to the 7th Army with all haste, we can be certain that the exhausted units of the 7th Army will, as happened south-west of Brussels, again be attacked, and this time completely beaten. This would mean that the strategic breach for which the enemy have been striving between the Maas and the Mosel would be opened up automatically, this time on the German frontier. I should like to stress at this point that when the 1st Army received timely reinforcements the situation improved for them considerably. If the same is to be done for the 7th Army it must be now or never.

I request that these conclusions, which have been made on reviewing the deteriorating situation, be brought to the notice of the Fuehrer.

Model, Field Marshal

✠

TO ARMY GROUP B, SEPTEMBER 15, 1944

The Army reports in connection with the disorders which took place at the evacuation of Aachen:

According to reports which came from the G.O.C., the Divisional Commander, the Battle Commandant, and the G2 of the Army, the blame lies incontestably with the Party officials entrusted with the evacuation. When the situation developed adversely, the responsible Party officials and the police, who alone could have kept peace and good order during the evacuation, hurriedly abandoned the city and tried to control the evacuation from the outside. Notice was given that every citizen who did not participate in the evacuation would be a traitor to his country, and this, coupled with the fact that there was no responsible local authority available, led to a panic, which developed into a headlong flight and universal looting.

As a result of the situation reported above in the city of Aachen, the commander of the 116th Panzer Division, Count Schwerin, took upon himself the duty of stopping the evacuation first of all, and then conducting it in a rational way. In doing this he disturbed the Aachen District Administrator by reporting that enemy attacking spearheads would probably be approaching the city by the afternoon. He has also given a letter to a member of the Party who had been named to him, in which he advised the population of Aachen, in English, to trust to the protection of the approaching American armies. Furthermore it has been clearly established that he had always taken all possible measures for the defense of Aachen, and that he has always commanded his division exactly as directed by the High Command.

Nevertheless, General Count Schwerin has been relieved of his post as Divisional Commander because of these mishaps. A court-martial enquiry has been started.

The Army Corps and Division immediately contacted the appropriate Party departments, and now everything has been done to control the evacuation according to plan.

> Brandenberger, General of Tank Forces
> 7th Army H. Q.

✠

TO C.-IN-C. WEST, FIELD MARSHAL VON RUNDSTEDT, SEPTEMBER 24, 1944

The position of Army Group B has become increasingly worse on the northern flank since the airborne landing on September 17, because the enemy succeeded in bringing in considerable reinforcements during daily flights. Our own reinforcements were insufficient. It was only possible to force a postponement of the enemy's operational intentions—a breakthrough via Eindhoven, Nijmegen and Arnhem, as a base for the attack on the Ruhr area—during the bitter fighting of the past few weeks, but apart from the holding of Arnhem, it was impossible to stop the enemy. The renewed airborne landing on September 23, the extent of which is not yet possible to judge, will lead to an exceptionally critical situation if we are not able to bring in adequate forces early enough to support the hard-pressed front line of the 1st Parachute Army.

The fact that the new landing took place on September 23, that is, 6 days after the first, suggests that the enemy had originally intended the landing on September 23 for another purpose, but now consider the time to be ripe to strengthen the present operation, obviously with the idea of turning to the south-east between the Rhine and the Maas. The danger is particularly great for this area, as there are no permanent defenses in the way of the presumed line of attack. Our own forces are inadequate against the enemy's continual push forward. New forces must be produced, or transferred from other fronts.

The quickest means of restoring the position would be an attack. That has been attempted in the direction of both Veghel and Nimegen. The forces available for the attack on Veghel proved to be insufficient for the task. Our pressure on Nijmegen could only be increased to an inadequate extent.

After yesterday's airborne landings—which the enemy could continue at any time—we cannot expect to be able to push the enemy back across the Waal, and so we must set up defenses in the region of the Lower Rhine on both sides of Arnhem.

The following consequences arise from this situation:

(1) The enemy resistance west of Arnhem must eventually be broken by all the means at our disposal, and the enemy must not be allowed to create a bridgehead to the northern bank of the Lower Rhine.

It will therefore be necessary to reinforce the II SS Panzer Corps with the 506th Tiger Detachment and the whole of the 246th Division.

(2) To release further forces, and to prevent the destruction of our formations, it may be necessary to withdraw the 15th

A German cross-Channel gun at Sangatte, near the port of Calais, on September 26, 1944. Although several port areas had been captured by this point, they had either been destroyed by retreating German forces or were too small to handle the volume of provisions needed by the four Allied armies which were now pursuing Army Group B toward Germany. The only suitable port, Antwerp, was captured on September 4 but could not be used until the surrounding Scheldt estuary was cleared. Bitter fighting in this area kept the area under German control until the end of November.

Army with the LXVII Army Corps into a bridgehead Bergen op Zoom–Roosendaal–Moerdijk, with the LXXXVIII Army Corps closing the gap on the left behind the Waal. Time could be found to put through this operation in spite of the fact that it would mean having to establish land communications with Walcheren in the event of penetration to the west, north of the Waal, by strong enemy motorized formations. The renewed danger of the encirclement of the 15th Army which this would entail could only be eliminated by bringing up strong reserves for the eastern flank of the Army. The conduct of battle of the 15th Army would therefore be such that the bridgehead could be held while preparations for a withdrawal were being made.

(3) While they are clearing up the position west of Arnhem and defending the present front east and south-east of Nijmegen, the 1st Parachute Army are so to direct their fighting on the left flank that a larger bridgehead can be held on the west bank of the Maas about 20 kilometers west of Venlo, from which it would be possible to launch an attack towards the north-west, after reinforcements had arrived. In view of the necessity for giving support at Arnhem and Nijmegen, forces for this bridgehead could only be obtained by introducing new units, or by withdrawing forces from the 7th Army.

The possibility of launching a larger counter-thrust from the sector of the 1st Parachute Army's left flank calls for examination of the question whether further forces (2 panzer divisions and 2 panzer brigades) could not be spared from other sectors for this operation.

It would be necessary to work very fast if we wished to make use of the enemy's present confinement in his corridor through Eindhoven. The 9th and 116th Panzer Divisions could be relieved by a good infantry division. Purely for defensive operations the following are needed:

1 infantry division
1 panzer division
1 panzer brigade.

(4) The 7th Army are still defending their present positions, and are preparing for a counter-attack to clear the enemy from the area east of Aachen. Before the 9th and the 116th Panzer Divisions could be released they would need an infantry division, and a further infantry division would be needed to replace the 2 panzer divisions from I SS Panzer Corps. If the 9th and 116th Panzer Divisions are used north-west of Venlo, another infantry division will be needed as rearguard in the Aachen district.

Altogether, if Army Group B is to continue a successful defensive action it will be required as a minimum:

(a) 2, or better, 3 infantry divisions for the 7th Army.

(b) 1 infantry division, 1 panzer division, a stronger panzer brigade for the 1st Parachute Army.

(c) 1 assault gun brigade each for the 15th Army, the 1st Parachute Army, and the 7th Army.

(d) Increased supplies of ammunition, especially for light and heavy field howitzers.

(e) Replacements for the infantry divisions at the points of heaviest fighting, at least 6 draft conducting battalions.

Model, Field Marshal

✠

TO C.-IN-C. WEST, FIELD MARSHAL VON RUNDSTEDT, SEPTEMBER 27, 1944

The fighting of Army Group B has suffered because of the following circumstances:

(1) Almost unlimited air superiority of the enemy.

The unsparing use of our fighter formations on various days has brought considerable temporary relief. In the main battle this relief is one of the first essentials for success. These experiences emphasize the necessity for producing the new fighter type as quickly as possible, even if it is at the expense of the bomber units.

(2) Superiority of the enemy artillery.

At the moment the Army Group has over 821 light and heavy cannon, some of them immobile. Against this the enemy artillery have at least 2,680 cannon. This discrepancy would not be so serious if we only had adequate supplies of ammunition. As this is not the case however, as is well known, the enemy's artillery superiority was more obvious. It is urgent that we have a speedy improvement in the supply either of ammunition or equipment, preferably of both.

(3) Preponderance of the enemy armored weapons.

At the present, our 239 tanks and assault guns are opposing 2,300 enemy tanks, i.e. 10 times the number. Moreover, this represents only half of the ascertained potential of enemy armored units. Even though the enemy have shown an unwillingness to use tank formations in close concentration during the past few days, there can still be no doubt whatsoever that they could throw in sudden concentrations of tanks at any time they wished. Therefore the request for increased supplies of assault gun brigades must be repeated. The formation and use of independent panzer brigades outside the framework of the panzer divisions has not been successful in the previous fighting. More adequate replacements for the tired panzer divisions, and the introduction of assault gun brigades and detachments form the most effective counter-measure against the enemy's panzer superiority.

It is an incontrovertible fact that the reverses in the west are primarily due to the panzer divisions having to fight when they were exhausted. The supply of equipment for them must be kept up.

(4) Insufficient replacements of personnel.

Even if the number of enemy infantry units is only $\frac{1}{3}$ higher than ours, the battle potential of our troops is lowered by their inadequate equipment, and by the fact that there are too many garrison and emergency units amongst our battalions.

During the period between September 1 and 25, our heavy losses were about 75,000 men; during the same period we received only 6,500 men as replacements. This intolerable discrepancy will eventually lead to the complete annihilation of whole valuable divisions, in spite of the plentiful use of newly constituted units. It is essential that we receive adequate numbers of replacements, so that it will be possible for the divisions to re-form their field relief battalions.

The Army Group will continue to try to withdraw in good time the units which have suffered very badly in the fighting, and form new units, as has already been done in the case of 14 divisions. The necessity for maintaining to some extent comparable and useful divisional strengths will mean that we will have to bring in garrison units.

I am reporting the foregoing points, although they are already known, because the result of the present decisive battles is dependent on their being given more consideration. I request that they may be brought directly to the notice of the Führer.

Model, Field Marshal

✠

TO ARMY GROUP B, SEPTEMBER 29, 1944

Estimate of the situation.
According to a verbal message from Reichsminister Speer, there is a factory in Weisweiler (4 kilometers east of Eschweiler) in which is made 40% of the total amount available of an alloy which is vital for the whole steel production.

Even if the present situation does not offer a direct threat to Weisweiler, it must still be emphasized that the defenses of the works, which lies only 6 kilometers behind the lines, are not sufficient to provide for the safety of the works in all circumstances. Apart from that, the works lie within range of effective enemy artillery fire.

In this respect also the situation demands that the enemy penetration east of Aachen be cleared up. The Army wishes to refer to the estimate of the situation dated September 23, 1944. In the first place the Army requests the bringing up of 2 panzer divisions to ensure the success of the proposed attack. If these cannot arrive within a short time, it will be considered necessary to have two complete attacking divisions, 1 Tiger or Panther detachment and sufficient assault guns (4 sections for the infantry divisions) or 2 brigades and H.Q. artillery (5–6 heavy

detachments). The need for sufficient ammunition is stressed.
In addition, the Army requests complete support in the formation now proceeding of a mortar battalion and an anti-tank
battalion, the personnel for which have been assembled and
armed by the Klosterkaemper Reception Unit, although their
lack of mobility and the shortage of optical instruments hin-
ders any rapid preparations.

Brandenberger
7th Army H.Q.

✠

TO C.-IN-C. WEST, OCTOBER 1, 1944

The following estimate of the situation is forwarded as an
appendix to the report already sent by courier:

The reports by our agents of the Americans bringing strong
reinforcements in the Aachen area, and of intended operations
directed against Cologne have not yet been confirmed by our
front line reconnaissance. The only indication which could
point to an intended attack has been the partial withdrawal by
1,000–1,500 meters of the most forward American positions in
the front of LXXXI Army Corps, as the enemy used a similar
method of leaving the ground open for bomber attacks on the
invasion front.

The general impressions of the enemy's movements, the
reports of prisoners, the scrutiny of captured documents,
artillery reconnaissance and reconnaissance by agents near the
front line have not so far supplied any other indications. Even
so, the Army is expecting the enemy to use the breach in the
West Wall around Aachen as a springing-off ground for a
breakthrough operation in the direction of Cologne and the
Ruhr industrial area. Therefore the Army is accordingly making its dispositions on the basis of the agents' reports.

In addition to the reinforcements for the defenses in the Aachen-Monschau area mentioned in the report dated September 30, 1944, the Army has ordered that an infantry battalion and the 341st Assault Gun Brigade (without the 2nd Battery) be transferred from LXXIV Army Corps, the 628th Mortar Detachment and the 1310th Fortress Artillery Detachment from I SS Panzer Corps, and the 2nd Battery of the 341st Assault Gun Brigade which is still with LXXX Army Corps. All of these units are to be transferred to LXXXI Army Corps by October 2. One of the draft conducting battalions formed by the Klosterkaemper Reception Unit and a mortar corps are also to be placed under the command of LXXXI Army Corps.

With regard to the munitions tactics, a definite concentration is being built up with LXXXI Army Corps. In addition the Army requests:

(1) Air reconnaissance in the area Liege-Amiens-Paris-Luxembourg.

(2) Luftwaffe support against the enemy artillery and prepared positions in the area of the breakthrough east and south-east of Aachen.

(3) A Tiger or Panther detachment to be brought in.

(4) The 7th Mortar Brigade which had already been promised to be brought in.

(5) The supply of a heavy artillery detachment with German guns.

(6) Adequate supplies of ammunition, with special reference to types of captured ammunition.

(7) The supply of medium mortars to take the place of the heavy and light mortars in the mortar battalion which is now being formed, as this is the only way of ensuring adequate supplies of ammunition.

(8) The Todt Organization to be persuaded to speed up the construction of an anti-tank front between Erkelenz and Dueren.

(9) Supplies of fuel to be sent to III Anti-aircraft Corps so that it will be possible to regroup the units with LXXXI

Army Corps, in accordance with the plan to concentrate forces there. Because we are so very short of fuel ourselves, it will not be possible for the Army to supply them with fuel.

Army Group B

✠

TO CHIEF OF OKW OPERATIONS STAFF, GENERAL JODL, OCTOBER 9, 1944

I request that the following estimate of the situation be submitted to the Führer:

I

(1) The point of greatest danger to the 15th Army is at the moment on their right flank in the area north of Antwerp, where the enemy is attempting to establish land connections with Walcheren.

With the enemy so strong in the area Nijmegen-Arnhem and near Aachen, it is not possible to withdraw further forces to help the 15th Army. Therefore the 15th Army must shorten its front between Tilburg and Bois-le-Duc, to release forces for the right wing.

The right flank of the 1st Parachute Army (XII SS Corps and II SS Panzer Corps) had to go over to the defensive. The situation around Aachen may make it necessary to remove troops from II SS Panzer Corps and send them there. I therefore request permission to give up the Arnhem bridgehead.

(2) The most dangerous point on the whole western front is on the right flank of the 7th Army, where there is a definite threat of encirclement to the whole area around Aachen. The bringing up of reinforcements is being continually slowed down by the regular destruction of railways, so that, for example, the heavy Panzer Detachment 506 (Tiger) has still not

A German gun position of the Atlantic Wall captured by Allied troops. In early September as the Germans retreated from the Seine, Allied intelligence reports assumed that enemy forces were diminished to the point that victory might come by Christmas. Instead, Army Group B had re-grouped by the end of September, with the 9th SS and 10th SS scoring a major victory against Operation MARKET GARDEN while the German Fifteenth Army held down Allied forces in the Antwerp area and the Fifth and Sixth Panzer and Seventh Armies stopped the American advance in southwestern Germany. Army Group B had performed its "Miracle in the West"; now Hitler and von Rundstedt turned to their plans for the Ardennes counteroffensive arrived at Aachen, the 3rd Panzer Grenadier Division will have to be diverted through Kaiserslauten, and so on. It is estimated that the enemy already have a superiority of 6 infantry divisions and 3 panzer divisions near Aachen, and it is possible that more forces will be sent up (American XXVII Army Corps). In spite of all endeavors, it does not seem as though we will be able to push back the enemy bulges in the front to the north and south-east of Aachen. There is an ever increasing danger that the enemy will be able to draw the circle more tightly round the town. I have issued clear instruction that Aachen is to be defended right to the very last, in agreement with the Fuehrer's orders. In this case, the possibility of the loss of the 246th Infantry Division must be accepted.

II

In the Army Group G area the enemy is seeking to invest Metz from the south, and to seize the Vosges passes by an attack on a broad front between Luneville and Lure. As yet there is no indication that there will definitely be an attack on the Burgundy Gate. It will be the task of Army Group G to offer stubborn resistance and thus gain enough time for the further building up of the Vosges positions. In this connection it may be deemed necessary to withdraw the bridgehead at Metz back to the Mosel.

III

The main factor which made it possible for the enemy to gain his recent successes (breakthrough at Eindhoven, gaining the northern bank of the Waal at Nijmegen, pincers movement on Aachen, etc.), is our shortage of reserves for counter-attacking. This shortage made it impossible to form concentrated defenses in time, even at the points where it was obvious that there was going to be a concentrated attack.

There is already a shortage of troops at the parts of the front line which have not yet been attacked, between Monschau and Diedenhof. The 48th Infantry Division was replaced there by the

416th Division, which has had no battle experience, and units of the 19th Infantry Division were removed (for the southern-flank of the 1st Army), so all that remains is a defense garrison under command of the divisional staffs. Considering the low battle potential of the defense battalions it would in my opinion be fatal to remove from the area around Trier the 36th Infantry Division, which is the only complete unit.

Just because I was so concerned about the shortage of reserves I requested that a reinforced regimental group be sent from each of the first 3 available infantry divisions. I now ask in addition for an infantry division to be sent from the assembly areas on each of the three dates, October 12, 15 and 18.

It would be possible to post relief detachments in northern Holland in place of the 256th and 361st Peoples' Grenadier Divisions. After the experiences of Nijmegen and Arnhem it is not very likely that the enemy will attempt any airborne landings east of the general line connecting Emden and Hamm. However the area west of this line is in great danger. And yet we have no great amount of reserves there.

I therefore request that the reinforcement of the 6th Panzer Army in the area Enschede-Borken-Haltern-Hamm-Muenster-Rheine be done especially early. From that area the Army can if required counter-attack at once in a north-west, west, or south-west direction.

My detailed requirements, once again, are: —

(a) Accelerated arrival of at least 7 draft conducting battalions (4 for Army Group B, 3 for Army Group G)

(b) Greater supplies of anti-tank weapons and materials.

(c) Further increase in ammunition allocations so that with an increased firing power, we will be able to approximate to the enemy strength.

C.-in-C. West Field Marshal von Rundstedt

TO C.-IN-C. WEST, FIELD MARSHAL VON RUNDSTEDT, OCTOBER 11, 1944

I wish to report that the situation at Aachen has become more critical. In spite of all our efforts the enemy succeeded in narrowing the corridor on both sides of Haaren to 3,000 meters.

This unfortunate development is mainly the direct result of the complete lack of replacements for the divisions which for several weeks have been in the thick of the fighting.

I request that representations be made to the Fuehrer of the urgency of providing as quickly as possible relief in the form of at least 1 draft conducting battalion for the 183rd and 246th Peoples' Grenadier Divisions, as well as for the 12th Division, since otherwise these divisions will be exhausted and it will be impossible to avoid further reverses.

The bitter and necessarily costly fighting against the enemy's large supplies of men and materials cannot possibly be continued without regular replacements.

Model, Field Marshal

APPENDIX 1

German Commander Biographies

SUPREME COMMAND OF THE ARMED FORCES (OKW: OBERKOMMANDO DER WEHRMACHT)

Keitel, Wilhelm

Field Marshal Wilhelm Keitel was OKW Chief of Staff. Along with Jodl and Warlimont, he relayed Hitler's orders to commanders in the field and conveyed their messages to Hitler, usually in the gentlest way possible. Over the course of the war, OKW became a rubber stamp for Hitler, a travelling headquarters that followed the Führer wherever he went. It oversaw operational planning, foreign intelligence, supply, and a wide variety of general concerns and problems. Keitel was noted for his ability to say what Hitler wanted to hear and for keeping unpleasant news from the Führer. He had been a staff officer since 1915 and after the Nazis came to power Keitel received promotions by remaining attached to Hitler. His obsequious ways were detested by many who had to deal with him, notably von Rundstedt, and Keitel's role as "Hitler's man" probably accounted for the fact that he held his position until the end of the war. On May 8, 1945, Keitel ratified the final German surrender. He was later executed on October 15, 1946, following his trial at Nuremburg.

Jodl, Alfred

As Keitel's deputy, Colonel General Alfred Jodl was OKW Chief of Operations. His primary function was to translate

Hitler's strategic orders into writing. Jodl had been at Hitler's side since 1940 and, like Keitel, was noted for the talent of being able to tell the Führer bad, often catastrophic, news from the battlefield while at the same time minimizing the fall-out from Hitler's temper. As a highly competent staff officer, Hitler's confidant, and top advisor at the Wolf's Lair, he was considered by many to be the most important man at OKW. As with Keitel, he rose through a succession of staff appointments, and to the bitter end Jodl was unshakably loyal to Hitler, to the extent that he was often indifferent to the ideas and demands of field commanders. Keitel and Jodl remained at the head of OKW until the German surrender, a remarkable fact in light of the firings and suicides witnessed in the latter part of the war. Jodl signed the Instrument of Surrender on May 7, 1945. At his execution in Nuremburg, he quietly uttered, "I greet you, oh my Germany."

Warlimont, Walter

General of Artillery Walter Warlimont was Jodl's Deputy Chief of Operations. On August 2, 1944, he was sent to Army Group B Headquarters to personally deliver Hitler's plans for Operation LÜTTICH, the counterattack that took place the following week at Mortain. In addition, he was being sent to keep an eye on von Kluge, whom Hitler was beginning to suspect of disloyalty. Opposition to LÜTTICH by the field commanders, von Kluge, Hausser, Eberbach, and Deitrich, was unanimous. Warlimont insisted that the commanders were to hold with determination; no retreat could be considered. He later signaled Hitler: "Everyone here confident of success." At this stage of the war, it would be suicidal to tell the Führer what he did not want to hear. Warlimont suffered severe injuries in the July 20 attempt on Hitler's life and thus was not with the OKW entourage in Berlin at the end of the war. After the surrender, Warlimont was taken prisoner by American forces.

COMMANDER-IN-CHIEF WEST
(OB WEST: OBERBEFEHLSHABER WEST)

Rundstedt, Gerd von

Field Marshal Gerd von Rundstedt commanded the German West Army, with sixty divisions under his command as of June 6, 1944. Rommel's Army Group B was stationed in Holland, Belgium, and northern France, and included the Fifteenth Army along the Channel coast east of the Seine as well as the Seventh Army between the Seine and the Loire Rivers. Von Blaskowitz's Army Group G was stationed in Southern France, with the First and Nineteenth Armies. Considered "trustworthy" by Hitler, von Rundstedt was recalled from retirement twice, first in 1939 as commander of Army Group South for the Polish and Russian campaigns, and again in 1942, at age sixty-four, as C-in-C West. He held this position almost until the end of the war, excluding the period from July 7 to September 5, 1944, during which time Field Marshals von Kluge and Model replaced him as C-in-C West. Von Rundstedt was an old-guard Prussian officer and a respected strategist, but he held no illusions regarding his army's ability to repel a massive invasion by an enemy whose main point of assault could not be determined in advance with any degree of certainty. He was enraged on D-Day by Hitler's delay in releasing the OKW reserves. At the height of the battle for Normandy, Hitler's conviction that the aging Field Marshal no longer held faith in ultimate victory led to von Rundstedt's replacement by von Kluge. He was later reinstated as C-in-C West on September 5, freeing up Model to assume command of Army Group B for the remainder of the campaign in northwest Europe. Von Rundstedt retired on March 11, 1945, and was replaced by Kesselring.

Kluge, Günther von

Field Marshal Hans Günther von Kluge replaced von Rundstedt as C-in-C West on July 7, 1944, and later took command of Army Group B as well after Rommel was critically injured on

July 17. Von Kluge had been a favorite of Hitler when he commanded Army Group Center in Russia, where he succeeded in developing lines of defense that held for two years. His messages were often passed directly to Hitler. "Clever Hans" arrived in France with high spirits, intending to make the counterattack that von Rundstedt was unable to pull together. He soon became disillusioned, however, to the point where he sent a brutally frank message to Hitler on August 3 outlining the dire consequences that would result from the implementation of Operation LÜTTICH. He showed some support for the July 20 conspirators, but ultimately refused to act against the Führer when the time came. After the assassination attempt, von Kluge fell under suspicion of complicity with the plot and was also believed to be trying to negotiate a surrender agreement with the Allies when he went "missing" on August 15. When Hitler appointed Model to replace von Kluge, the latter committed suicide before he could be recalled to Berlin. He left a final letter for Hitler, protesting his undying loyalty to the Führer and urging him to negotiate peace if his counteroffensive did not bring victory. Hitler, unimpressed, denied von Kluge any military honors at his funeral.

Model, Walter
Recognized as "Hitler's Fireman" and a master of defensive operations, Field Marshal Walter Model commanded Army Groups North and South on the Eastern Front and, in June 1944, brought the Soviet drive against Army Group Center to a halt outside Warsaw. On August 17, 1944, he was transferred to Normandy to replace von Kluge as C-in-C West, at which point he also took command of Army Group B in Rommel's absence. Model worked his men hard, but only within the limits of what was possible. He was replaced by von Rundstedt as C-in-C West on September 5, but stayed on as the commander of Army Group B to coordinate the German defense against Allied airborne landings at Arnhem. He later helped to plan the Ardennes offensive. Towards the end of the war, Model was

trapped in the Rühr pocket with his 200,000-man force. Having let Hitler down, Model drew his Luger and shot himself in the head.

Blumentritt, Günther

Major General Günther Blumentritt was Chief of Staff to von Rundstedt, von Kluge, and Model at OB West headquarters in St-Germain. Before dawn on June 6, 1944, in Rommel's absence, Blumentritt called Jodl at Berchtesgaden requesting permission to move the Panzer Lehr Division to the beaches, but was told to wait until daylight reconnaissance clarified the situation. On August 2, Blumentritt met with Warlimont to receive the plans for Operation LÜTTICH and was angered by the unrealistic objectives of the Mortain offensive. Warlimont repeated the official line: There would be no retreat; the lines would be held with fanatical determination.

HEADQUARTERS, ARMY GROUP B

Rommel, Erwin

A skilled tactician and dynamic leader, Field Marshal Erwin Rommel was C-in-C of Army Group B, tasked with defeating any attempted landing by the Allies in northern France. From his headquarters at La Roche–Guyon, Rommel worked feverishly during the spring of 1944 to fortify the Atlantic Wall. He shared Hitler's views that it was necessary to create an impenetrable coastal defense network that would halt and defeat invading forces on the beaches before they had a chance to gain a foothold on the continent.

Prior to his assignment in Normandy, Rommel had earned great fame and respect as the "Desert Fox" of the North African campaign, fighting against Montgomery's Eighth Army. He conducted two major offensive drives with his Afrika Korps before being defeated at El Alamein. He then directed an extended fighting retreat to Tunisia and became the youngest field marshal in German history at age fifty. In Normandy, however, Rommel became increasingly disillusioned with Hitler and frequently burst out to his staff, "The man is mad!" When von Rundstedt was dismissed in July 1944, Hitler passed over Rommel and instead promoted von Kluge, a man who Rommel viewed as self-serving and pompous. He believed the Führer was dragging Germany down with him, mindlessly butchering a generation of young men. Much of Rommel's control over the armies and panzer groups of Army Group B was diminished by Hitler's decision to place reserve divisions under his own control, other mobile reserves under von Rundstedt, and still other divisions in Normandy under Rommel.

On July 17, Rommel's car was driven off the road by Allied aircraft and he suffered severe injuries that necessitated his evacuation from Normandy. While recovering in Germany, he was implicated in the July 20 plot by a delirious von Stülpnagel. On October 14, Hitler's agents gave Rommel a choice of taking poison or being brought up on charges at a public trial, thereby putting his family at risk as well. Rommel chose suicide by poison. Hitler avoided any public reaction by giving Rommel a full state funeral. Officially, Rommel had died from his wounds from the car crash in Normandy.

Speidel, Hans

Lieutenant General Hans Speidel was Chief of Staff, Army Group B, serving under Rommel and later von Kluge and Model. On D-Day, with Rommel in Germany, Dollmann of the Seventh Army at Rennes for war games, and Dietrich in Belgium, Speidel was the acting commander at Army Group B Headquarters. Speidel was noted as a brilliant and capable general, but as senior staff officer he could not speak with the same authority as Rommel. At midnight on 6 June, he alerted von Rundstedt's headquarters and the Fifteenth Army to the Allied landings. Holding a Ph.D. in philosophy, the precise and analytical Speidel was an ardent supporter of Rommel and was arrested by the Gestapo after the July 20 plot as an active conspirator. After the war, he went on to become the commander of NATO forces in Western Europe.

ARMY COMMANDERS, ARMY GROUP B

Hausser, Paul

SS General Paul Hausser replaced Colonel General Friedrich Dollmann as commander of Seventh Army after the latter's death on June 29, 1944, which was officially reported by Speidel as a heart-attack but is generally thought to have been a suicide by cyanide capsule. Hausser had already gained fame as commander of the II SS Panzer Corps. In Normandy, Hausser's Seventh Army faced bitter fighting against American forces during the Operation COBRA breakout at the end of July. Hausser was subsequently caught in the Falaise pocket and badly wounded by shrapnel to his face on August 19, 1944. He was later able to escape through the Falaise Gap along with many of his troops. After the Battle of Normandy, Eberbach replaced Hausser as commander of the Seventh Army.

Geyr von Schweppenburg, Leo

Field Marshal Baron Leo Geyr von Schweppenburg commanded Panzer Group West, later designated the Fifth Panzer Army. He was a strong supporter of von Rundstedt in his dispute with Rommel over the deployment of reserve armored forces, believing that a concentrated mobile panzer reserve was the best defense against the inevitable Allied landings, wherever they might fall. Baron von Schweppenburg was wounded on June 11, 1944, when the location of his headquarters was identified by ULTRA and subsequently bombed by Allied aircraft. On July 1, 1944, Rommel informed Geyr von Schweppenburg that he and von Rundstedt were being relieved of command, and to this Rommel added that he himself would likely be the next to go. General Eberbach took over command of the Fifth Panzer Army from July 2 to August 19.

Eberbach, Heinrich

A veteran tank commander, General of Panzer Troops Heinrich Eberbach took over Panzer Group West from Geyr von Schweppenburg on July 2, arriving at his new post with high hopes of turning the battle of Normandy around. By mid-July, he had prepared the strongest defensive line yet established in Normandy in order to counter the British breakout attempt at Caen (Operation GOODWOOD). He was dismayed when War-limont delivered plans for the Mortain counteroffensive to him on August 3. Eberbach knew that if the plan failed his Panzer divisions would likely become trapped inside an Allied pocket. Eberbach took command of the Seventh Army when Hausser was injured at Falaise on August 19, and was, in turn, replaced by Dietrich, who assumed command of the Fifth Panzer Army. Eberbach, along with his Headquarters, was captured by the British 3rd Royal Tank Regiment at Amiens on August 31, 1944. General of Tank Forces Brandenberger then took command of the Seventh Army.

Dietrich, Joseph "Sepp"

Commander of I SS Panzer Corps, Colonel General Joseph "Sepp" Dietrich had been a favourite of Hitler's since the early days of the Nazi regime. In 1933 he formed the elite *Leibstandarte* division, Hitler's personal bodyguard unit. Early in the war, as a reward for loyal service to the Nazi party, Dietrich was appointed to a senior rank in the Waffen-SS. Both Rommel and von Rundstedt gravely doubted his qualifications as a field commander.[1] Dietrich's I SS Panzer Corps helped pin-down Montgomery's 21st Army Group outside Caen for over a month after the D-Day landings. He then took command of the Fifth Panzer Army when Eberbach left to replace Hausser in the Seventh Army. Dietrich opposed the plans for Operation LÜTTICH when they were delivered to him on August 3 by Warlimont, fearing that moving his panzer divisions to the Mortain-Avranches area would leave Caen critically weakened. Dietrich later said, "There was only one person to blame for this stupid, impossible operation. That madman Adolf Hitler. It was a Führer order. What else could we do?"[2] By August 13, Dietrich sent a desper-

---

[1] D'Este, 168.

[2] D'Este, 460.

ate warning to von Kluge that British and American troops would soon surround the Fifth Panzer and Seventh Armies. German forces in the developing encirclement would have to withdraw before their supply of ammunition and fuel was cut off and it became possible for the enemy to fire into the pocket from all directions. Dietrich took command of the Fifth Panzer Army a few days later, replacing Eberbach.

DIVISION COMMANDERS, ARMY GROUP B

Bayerlein, Fritz

Lieutenant General Fritz Bayerlein commanded the 130th "Panzer Lehr," a demonstration division formed to combat the expected Allied invasion and one of the strongest divisions in the German Army. Stationed in Le Mans, Panzer Lehr was finally able to mobilize late on June 6 after Hitler authorized the release of OKW reserves to the Normandy front. The next day, along with the 12th SS "Hitler Youth," it came to the aid of Feuchtinger's 21st Panzer Division, which had already been brought into action on D-Day near Caen. Bayerlein's division helped halt Montgomery's advance outside Caen, but at a terrible cost. Panzer Lehr bore the brunt of U.S. Operation COBRA, leaving this once-elite division on the verge of destruction after a massive aerial bombardment on July 25, 1944, in support of the American breakout. On August 13, Bayerlein was wounded in the Falaise pocket near Argentan.

Feuchtinger, Edgar

At the head of the reconstructed 21st Panzer Division was Lieutenant General Edgar Feuchtinger. The original 21st Division had been part of Rommel's Afrika Korps and was partially destroyed at El Alamein and finished off during the fall of Tunisia. The new division was put together from scratch, largely through the energy and efficiency of Feuchtinger. With a cadre of 3,000 men, he gathered tanks and armored vehicles from German scrapyards. By the spring of 1944 it was a powerful force consisting of three panzer regiments, two panzer-grenadier regiments, and support units totaling 16,000 men.

Feuchtinger, who assisted with the Nazi party's Nuremburg rallies prior to the war, was a favorite of Adolf Hitler. He was a close friend of Rommel and a strong supporter of his Atlantic Wall static defense system. In late May 1944, the 21st Panzer Division moved south of Caen. It was positioned near the coast for the D-Day landings and was the only panzer division to mount a counterattack against the Allies on June 6, thereby helping to prevent the fall of Caen. After the retreat through France, Feuchtinger's division was assigned to Army Group G and served in the southern sector of the western front.

Schwerin, Gerhard von

Lieutenant General Count Gerhard von Schwerin commanded the 116th Panzers, known as the "Greyhound Division" due to the speed with which it moved in 1943 to rescue German divisions trapped on the Russian front. In 1944, Count von Schwerin had become the third general in the Wehrmacht to be awarded the Knight's Cross of the Iron Cross with Oak Leaves and Swords. Hitler praised him as a splendid battlefield commander, despite the fact that von Schwerin was not a Nazi. His 116th Division took part in the counterattack at Mortain and was later caught in the Falaise pocket, where it broke out through the Gap with heavy losses. One of the German Army's most decorated generals, Count von Schwerin had by this time lost all hope for victory. Had the July 20 plot succeeded, von Schwerin was to be chosen as an emissary to approach the Anglo-American leadership and negotiate a truce on behalf of the rebellious generals in the West. On August 7, 1944, he was relieved of his command by Hausser for refusing to carry out an order to engage the 116th Division on the right flank of LÜTTICH. Von Schwerin was later re-appointed to his command, but in mid-September, while the 116th was in action at Aachen, he ordered an unauthorized retreat from the city and was once again relieved—this time by Hitler and therefore permanently.

Meyer, Kurt

On June 17, 1944, Major General Kurt Meyer took command of the 12th SS Panzers, the "Hitler Youth" Division. At age thirty-three, Meyer was the youngest divisional commander in the German armed forces. He had joined the SS at a young age under the sponsorship of Dietrich in the *Leibstandarte* Division. He was recognized for his accomplishments in the Balkans and Russia before being appointed second-in-command of the newly formed 12th SS. The "Hitler Youth" Division had a fierce reputation as the most fanatical unit in the German army, having been recruited in 1943 from the Hitler Youth Movement. Its elite soldiers were all between sixteen and eighteen years old, specially chosen for their aptitude and enthusiasm. The 12th SS came into action against the Allied bridgehead in Normandy on June 7. Although Meyer was still a colonel at the time, he took command of the division after its commander, General Witt, was killed. Meyer established his headquarters at the Abbaye Ardennes, where the 12th SS gained notoriety for murdering Canadian prisoners of war. The 12th SS acted as a rear-guard during the German evacuation of Caen, and was noted for its determined stand on the outskirts of the city. The 12th SS Panzers helped keep the "neck" of the Falaise Gap open, allowing remnants of the Seventh and Fifth Panzer Armies to escape. In September 1944, Meyer was wounded and captured in Belgium and was later tried for the murder of Canadian POWs by troops under his command.

Zangen, Gustav-Adolf von

In 1943, General of the Infantry Gustav-Adolf von Zangen was appointed General Officer Commanding of the 17th Division. He was later promoted to the command of LXXXIV Corps and then of LXXXVII Corps. In Italy during 1943–44 he was GOC of Army Detachment von Zangen, and later commanded the Lower Alps Zone. On August 27, 1944, he replaced von Salmuth as commander of the Fifteenth Army and a few days later, after the closing of the Falaise Gap, von Zangen was given responsibility for defending the Channel coast from the

Seine to the Scheldt estuary. On September 4, his forces became encircled after the fall of Antwerp, but a difficult evacuation across the Scheldt beginning on September 6 rescued 90,000 men of the Fifteenth Army along with their vehicles, equipment, and horses.[3] Completing the evacuation by September 23, von Zangen's divisions reached Arnhem just in time to strengthen the right wing of the German defenses facing the Allied Operation MARKET GARDEN.

---

[3] Stacey, 303; OKW, 190.

APPENDIX 2

German Army Order of Battle

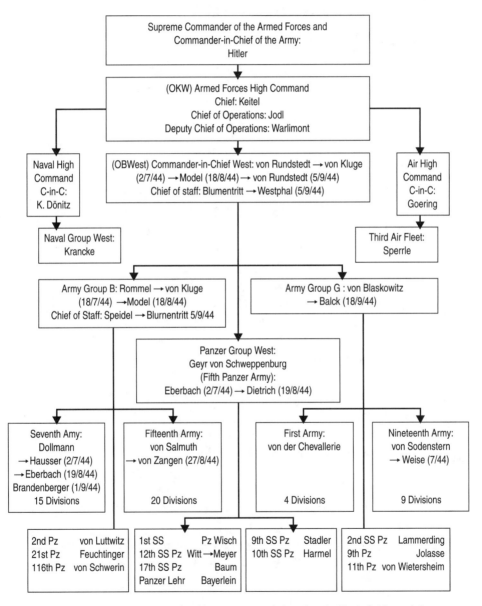

```
Supreme Commander of the Armed Forces and
Commander-in-Chief of the Army:
Hitler
```

```
(OKW) Armed Forces High Command
Chief: Keitel
Chief of Operations: Jodl
Deputy Chief of Operations: Warlimont
```

```
Naval High
Command
C-in-C:
K. Dönitz
```

```
(OBWest) Commander-in-Chief West: von Rundstedt → von Kluge
(2/7/44) → Model (18/8/44) → von Rundstedt (5/9/44)
Chief of staff: Blumentritt → Westphal (5/9/44)
```

```
Air High
Command
C-in-C:
Goering
```

```
Naval Group West:
Krancke
```

```
Third Air Fleet:
Sperrle
```

```
Army Group B: Rommel → von Kluge
(18/7/44) → Model (18/8/44)
Chief of Staff: Speidel → Blurnentritt 5/9/44
```

```
Army Group G : von Blaskowitz
→ Balck (18/9/44)
```

```
Panzer Group West:
Geyr von Schweppenburg
(Fifth Panzer Army):
Eberbach (2/7/44) → Dietrich (19/8/44)
```

```
Seventh Amy:
Dollmann
→ Hausser (2/7/44)
→ Eberbach (19/8/44)
Brandenberger (1/9/44)
15 Divisions
```

```
Fifteenth Army:
von Salmuth
→ von Zangen (27/8/44)


20 Divisions
```

```
First Army:
von der Chevallerie



4 Divisions
```

```
Nineteenth Army:
von Sodenstern
→ Weise (7/44)


9 Divisions
```

2nd Pz	von Luttwitz
21st Pz	Feuchtinger
116th Pz	von Schwerin

1st SS	Pz Wisch
12th SS Pz	Witt →Meyer
17th SS Pz	Baum
Panzer Lehr	Bayerlein

| 9th SS Pz | Stadler |
| 10th SS Pz | Harmel |

2nd SS Pz	Lammerding
9th Pz	Jolasse
11th Pz	von Wietersheim

Note: Panzer Divisions were transferred between commands throughout the May to October period.

APPENDIX 3

Chronology of Army Group B from Normandy to the West Wall

MAY

7 High Command Instruction confirms Hitler's assignment of three Panzer Divisions to Rommel, three to C-in-C West and four to strategic OKW reserve under Hitler's control

9 Rommel arrives to assume command at La Roche–Guyon, Army Group B Headquarters

10 Rommel sends message to OKW warning of seriousness of locomotive situation: forced labor and even POWs will have to be used at repair shops

15 Montgomery presents final plans for Operation OVERLORD at St. Paul's, London

15 Double-agent "Arabel" informs by German High Command of "Armee Gruppe Patton" units stationed in southeast England

19 Rommel sends message reporting that he is short of tanks, officers, motor transport and vehicle spares

20 Rommel's requests to place a second panzer division near St. Lô and to have the Bay of Seine mined are refused: Hitler is convinced that the main invasion will be in Calais area

21 A report from von Rundstedt's Headquarters anticipates that the Allies will mount several simultaneous assaults and use new weapons for their invasion

21 Systematic Allied aircraft attacks against French bridges, tunnels, rail lines, rolling stock, power stations, marshalling and repair yards begin

25 Decrypted German Air Force Enigma messages show the Allied invasion is expected in the Dieppe area

26 Allies launch a daylight raid on Lyons to block German reinforcement routes from the south

27 ULTRA decrypts alert Allies of German troop build-up in the Cotentin Peninsula

28 Second U.S. bomber raid sent against German synthetic oil plants; wireless station near Bruges is destroyed

31 V-1 Flying bomb sites are attacked by Allies; two-thirds are put out of action

JUNE

1 French Resistance receives the first coded message from the BBC signaling that the invasion is imminent

2 Von Rundstedt receives a signal from Berlin that the Allies will need four consecutive days of good weather for a cross-channel assault. No such clear spell is forecast

3 De Gaulle announces from Algeria that his provisional government will replace the Vichy Cabinet as soon as the Allies liberate France from Nazi rule

4 Stormy forecast: Eisenhower postpones D-Day from June 5 to June 6

4 Rommel travels to Germany for his wife's birthday and to meet with Hitler

5 Hitler receives news that the Allies have taken control of Rome

5 Stormy weather is predicted to continue. War Games are held at Rennes with most of the Seventh Army's senior officers attending

5 Close to midnight the Allies carry out various radar deceptions to mask the landings of the 101st and 82nd Airborne troops in Normandy

6 D-Day: Allies lands troops at Utah, Omaha, Gold, Juno, and Sword beaches

6 OKW denies von Rundstedt's request to release the Panzer reserves. Jodl decides not to awaken Hitler until it is certain that the Normandy invasion is the main attack

6 Feuchtinger mobilizes his 21st Panzer Division in the afternoon as Rommel races back to Normandy under Hitler's orders to drive the enemy back into the sea by midnight

7 Panzer Lehr and the 12th SS Panzer Divisions come into action. Bayeux falls as Allied landings are reported to be successful along a fifty-mile front

8 First U.S. (Omaha) and Second British (Gold) Armies link up near Port-en-Bessin

10 2nd SS "Das Reich" Division kills 642 civilians in Oradour-sur-Glane in reprisals to the French Resistance

11 Geyr von Schweppenburg is wounded and seventeen staff officers killed in the bombing of Panzer Group West Headquarters at La Caine

11 Rommel concentrates four Panzer divisions around Caen: 21st, 2nd, 12th SS, and Panzer Lehr

12 American march toward Cherbourg begins as U.S. forces capture Carentan

13 V-1 Flying bomb offensive is launched against London— six civilians are killed

13 Four German Tiger tanks check the British 17th Armoured Division at Villers-Bocage

15 Second V-1 raid on London—more than fifty civilians are killed

16 The Great Storm begins over the English Channel

17 Hitler meets with Rommel and von Rundstedt at Margival near Soissons

17 Kurt Meyer is appointed to command the 12th SS Division. At age thirty-three, he is the youngest divisional commander in the German Armed Forces

17 "Arabel" is awarded the Iron Cross with Hitler unaware that he is a double-agent

18 U.S. VII Corps reaches Barneville at the west coast of the Cotentin Peninsula

19 Loss of the American Mulberry harbour and damage to the British Mulberry at Arromanches during the Great Storm increases the importance of capturing Cherbourg

20 Bad weather allows reinforcement of the Normandy defenses by the 9th SS and 10th SS Panzer Divisions from Poland, 1st SS Panzer from the north, and 2nd SS Panzer from southern France

20 Churchill instructs Special Operations Executive to fly in whatever is needed in arms and ammunition to assist the French Resistance movement

22 Third anniversary of the German invasion of the Soviet Union. Red Army's summer offensive opens along a 300-mile front against Army Group Center

23 The 2nd SS Panzer Division arrives in Normandy, having taken seventeen days to move from its base in Toulouse, normally a three-day journey. Sabotage by the French Resistance movement and the Allied bombing campaign slowed its advance

25 The suburbs of Cherbourg are stormed by U.S. troops

26 Hitler wires von Schlieben to hold Cherbourg to the last cartridge. Following vicious street fighting in the evening, von Schlieben is forced to surrender what is left of the garrison

26 Montgomery launches Operation EPSOM, his third attempt to take Caen, with a major offensive across the Odon River

29 At a meeting with von Rundstedt and Rommel at Berchtesgaden, Hitler still ignores the advice of his field marshals that existing battle lines cannot be held. He refuses requests for extensive reinforcements and greater freedom of action in the field

JULY

1 Von Rundstedt receives notice that von Kluge will replace him as C-in-C West

1 Geyr von Schweppenburg is replaced by Eberbach as commander of Fifth Panzer Army

2 Hausser succeeds Dollmann as the commander of the Seventh Army

3 Arriving at Army Group B Headquarters at La Roche–Guyon to assume command, von Kluge believes he can save Normandy and berates Rommel for his defeatist attitude

5 Inexperienced 16th Luftwaffe Field Division takes over from the 21st Panzer Division near Caen

6 Churchill tells the House of Commons that of 2,754 V-1 flying bombs launched to date, 2,752 people have been killed

7 2,500 tons of bombs are dropped on Caen by British bombers; much of the city is destroyed

7 Rommel and von Kluge decide to shift Panzer Lehr Division to the American front

8 The 16th Luftwaffe Field Division collapses before British and Canadian forces at Caen in Operation CHARNWOOD

8 American forces seize La Haye-du-Puits

9 Battle for Caen ends with the Allies in control of the city and heavy casualties on both sides. The 12th SS remains in the outskirts to protect the retreat

10 Bradley decides to pause and rest U.S. troops while replacing their 40,000 Normandy casualties to date

11 Panzer Lehr comes into action against Bradley's troops. Bogged down in the *bocage* country, Bradley asks Montgomery to attack in the east while U.S. troops rebuild for a breakout campaign near St. Lô

15 Rommel writes a blunt report of conditions to von Kluge, requesting that it be forwarded to OKW. He notes that 97,000 casualties have been replaced by only 6,000 troops and that the Fifteenth Army is still needed in the Pas de Calais to defend against another landing. Operation FORTITUDE is still successful in diverting German forces to the north

16 Hitler refuses Rommel's request to release 28,000 troops from the Channel Islands to France

17 Rommel is critically injured in a car crash after a Spitfire attack near Ste. Foy de Montgommery

18 Eberbach's Fifth Panzer Army forms part of the defense against Montgomery's Operation GOODWOOD at the Orne River

18 Hitler agrees to move some mobile units to Normandy from the Pas de Calais

18 Americans capture St. Lô junction, a critical link between Normandy and Brittany

19 German armored units destined for the American front are switched back to the British-Canadian sector in anticipation of a breakout toward Paris

20 Von Stauffenberg places a bomb under the map table of the Wolf's Lair in an attempt to assassinate Hitler

20 Von Kluge delays in accepting the conspirators' orders upon hearing that the Führer survived the blast

21 Dietrich's Panzers stop Operation GOODWOOD near Troteval Farm. Verrières Ridge remains in German hands

22 Hitler wires his commanders that anyone who gives up an inch of ground will be shot

23 Hausser ignores von Kluge's order to put infantry on the front line and place tanks in reserve to the rear, leaving Bayerlein's Panzer Lehr in place

25 American Operation COBRA starts the U.S. breakout with intensive bombing of Panzer Lehr along the road between St. Lô and Périers

27 "Rhino" tanks assist American progress through the hedgerows. Périers falls

28 German lines begin to fall back as U.S. forces take Coutances

28 Von Kluge informs Jodl that everything is a gigantic mess, the front is collapsing before the U.S. advance

28 Hitler authorizes more divisions from the Fifteenth Army to move into Normandy

30 American forces "turn the corner" at Avranches

30 Patton's U.S. Third Army advances through Brittany while Hodges' U.S. First Army maintains pressure against Hausser's Seventh Army

30 Intense counterattacks follow the launch of British Operation BLUECOAT near Caumont

31 Von Kluge calls OKW to come to see conditions for themselves: "It's a madhouse here!"

AUGUST

1 Hitler orders von Aulock to fight to the last man as American and British bombers pound his forces at the old citadel in St. Malo

2 Warlimont flies from the Wolf's Lair carrying Hitler's plans for Operation LÜTTICH to OB-West Headquarters at St. Germain. Blumentritt is enraged by its unrealistic goals

3 Dietrich and Eberbach warn Warlimont of dire consequences of pulling SS divisions away from Caen for the Mortain counter-offensive

4 Warlimont signals Hiltler: "Everyone here confident of success."

4 Montgomery endorses Bradley's order for Patton to clear Brittany with minimum forces while others swing around behind the Fifth Panzer Army

5 Von Kluge sends a warning to Hitler that LÜTTICH will bring disaster; Hitler responds to proceed as ordered

5 Near midnight ULTRA alerts Bradley and Montgomery of Panzer divisions moving west

6 To date, Operation COBRA has destroyed nearly thirteen German divisions, including 250,000 casualties

6 Americans are close to all of Brittany's main ports

7 Hausser relieves von Schwerin from command of 116th Division for refusing orders to begin the attack at Mortain

7 Hitler finally releases the remainder of the Fifteenth Army to join the fight in Normandy: the hold of Operation FORTITUDE has ended

8 89th Infantry Division faces bombing as Operation TOTALIZE begins near Quesnay Wood

8 Fifth Panzer and Seventh Armies begin their retreat from the pocket created by fighting on both the Caen/Falaise and Avranches/Mortain fronts

9 Nineteen German divisions are concentrated between the Orne and Vire Rivers: ten near Caen are mainly infantry divisions and nine near Mortain are mainly Panzer

11 Dug-in Germans force a halt to Operation TOTALIZE. Montgomery orders Canadians to take Falaise and advance with the British toward U.S. forces at Argentan

11 Von Kluge meets with Hausser, Dietrich and Eberbach to get their agreement for a request to withdraw from Mortain

11 Hitler tells Warlimont the attack is failing because von Kluge wants it to. The renewal of the Führer's Operation LÜTTICH is cancelled

12 German advance is brought to a standstill outside Mortain; convoys are streaming east

12 Eberbach organizes a defense at Argentan to allow escape from the Falaise pocket

12 U.S. XV Corps takes Alençon

13 Dietrich sends a desperate message that if the front is not withdrawn immediately to move out of the threatened encirclement, all will be lost

14 85th Infantry and 12th SS Panzers face the Canadians as they drive toward Falaise in Operation TRACTABLE

15 Hitler's "worst day of the war" sees Allied forces land on the French Mediterranean coast, the Russian steamroller advancing at Ploesti, Falaise threatened, Alençon on the defensive, and von Kluge gone "missing"

16 Von Kluge is finally given permission to retreat through the Falaise Gap

17 Model arrives with orders from Hitler to assume command as C-in-C West. Von Kluge is recalled to Berlin and commits suicide on the way there

17 Von Aulock surrenders St. Malo to the Americans

18 Model orders Hausser's Seventh and Eberbach's Fifth Panzer Armies to be evacuated out of the pocket as soon

as possible. Tens of thousands escape eastward under steady bombardment

19 U.S. V Corps and Canadian II Corps join at Chambois to begin closing the Falaise Gap

19 Hausser is badly wounded while escaping the pocket. Eberbach assumes command of the Seventh Army while Dietrich takes over the Fifth Panzer Army

20 Aided by bad weather grounding aircraft, the escape of Army Group B continues. 50,000 have been taken prisoner and 10,000 killed while trapped in the Falaise pocket

24 Over the past five days 300,000 German soldiers have been ferried across the Seine

25 Von Choltitz surrenders Paris, ignoring orders to destroy the city if forced to retreat

27 Von Zangen assumes command of the Fifteenth Army to defend the Channel coast

28 Germans surrender Toulon and Marseilles in southern France

29 Americans close in on Bordeaux, the last German enclave in southern France

30 De Gaulle forms a provisional government in Paris

31 Eberbach is captured by British forces near Amiens

SEPTEMBER

1 American forces storm Sedan, enter Argonne; Canadians take Dieppe

2 Eisenhower orders U.S. First and Third Armies to halt due to fuel and supply problems

3 British troops liberate Brussels, greeted by exuberant celebrations

3 Americans capture Lyons in southern France

4 Von Zangen's army is enveloped as the port at Antwerp is captured by the British. The port will not be useable until both banks of the fifty-mile Scheldt Estuary are cleared.

5 Von Rundstedt arrives at Koblenz as C-in-C West, freeing up Model to command Army Group B in the battle for Belgium and Holland

5 Hitler orders von Zangen's Fifteenth Army across the Scheldt to the mainland to defend the Albert Canal line north of Antwerp.

6 Meyer is captured and wounded near Namur in south-east Belgium

7 The first V-2 rocket lands in London

11 The 2nd SS "Das Reich" Division takes up its position in the West Wall

13 A determined German defense faces the Battle for the Breskens Pocket

14 Bomber Command renews its air offensive against Germany

14 Belgium, Luxembourg and part of Holland have fallen to the Allies

15 Allied forces reach the West Wall between Aachen and Trier

16 Hitler presents his plans for the Ardennes Offensive

17 9th SS and 10th SS Panzer Divisions react quickly in checking Operation MARKET GARDEN

23 In a skillful retreat, von Zangen has evacuated 90,000 men, 600 guns and 6200 vehicles from Breskens to Walcheren Island. His divisions arrive to strengthen the Arnhem front

25 Allied troops are withdrawn from Arnhem following a disastrous campaign

26 Hitler signs a decree conscripting men aged from sixteen to sixty for a "People's Army"

OCTOBER

1 Canadians take Calais and overrun the V-1 flying bomb sites

4 The Fifteenth Army stands firm near Antwerp as the Battle for the Scheldt begins

5 U.S. advance is temporarily called to a halt due to supply line problems

6 German jet aircraft first used in battle over Nijmegen

10 85th Infantry Division "Battle Group Chill" arrives to hold the Walcheren Corridor
14 Implicated in the July 20 plot, Rommel commits suicide
18 Von Rundstedt enforces orders to build up defenses of the West Wall in preparation for Hitler's planned Ardennes offensive

Works Cited

Barnett, Corelli, ed. *Hitler's Generals.* New York: Grove Weidenfeld, 1989.

Blumenson, Martin. *Breakout and Pursuit.* United States Army in World War II Series: The European Theater of Operations. Washington, DC: Center of Military History, United States Army, 1989.

Bradley, Omar. *A Soldier's Story.* New York: Random House, 1999 [1951].

Copp, Terry. *Fields of Fire: The Canadians in Normandy.* Toronto: University of Toronto Press, 2003.

Copp, Terry, and Robert Vogel. *Maple Leaf Route: Falaise, Antwerp & Scheldt.* Alma, ON: Maple Leaf Route, 1987.

D'Este, Carlo. *Decision in Normandy.* New York: Koncky & Konecky, 1994 [1983].

Gilbert, Martin. *Second World War.* New Edition. London: Phoenix Press, 2000 [1989].

Harrison, Gordon A. *Cross-Channel Attack.* United States Army in World War II Series: The European Theater of Operations. Washington, DC: Center of Military History, United States Army, 1989.

Hastings, Max. *Overlord: D-Day and the Battle for Normandy.* New York: Simon & Schuster, 1984.

Hinsley, F. H., et al. *British Intelligence in the Second World War: Its Influence on Strategy and Operations.* Vol. 3, Pt. 2. London: Her Majesty's Stationery Office, 1988.

Keegan, John. *Six Armies in Normandy.* New York: Viking-Penguin, 1982.

OKW. "War Diary (1 Apr–18 Dec 1944)." MS# B-034. In *World War II: German Military Studies.* Vol. 10, Pt. 4. New York: Garland Publishing, 1979.

Overy, Richard. *Why the Allies Won.* New York: W. W. Norton & Company, 1995.

Stacey, C. P. *The Victory Campaign. The Operations in North-West Europe 1944–1945.* Vol. 3, Official History of the Canadian Army in the Second World War. Ottawa: The Queen's Printer and Controller of Stationery, 1960.

Weigley, Russell. *Eisenhower's Lieutenants: The Campaign of France and Germany, 1944–1945.* Indianapolis: Indiana University Press, 1990 [1981].

Index

Stackpole Military History Series

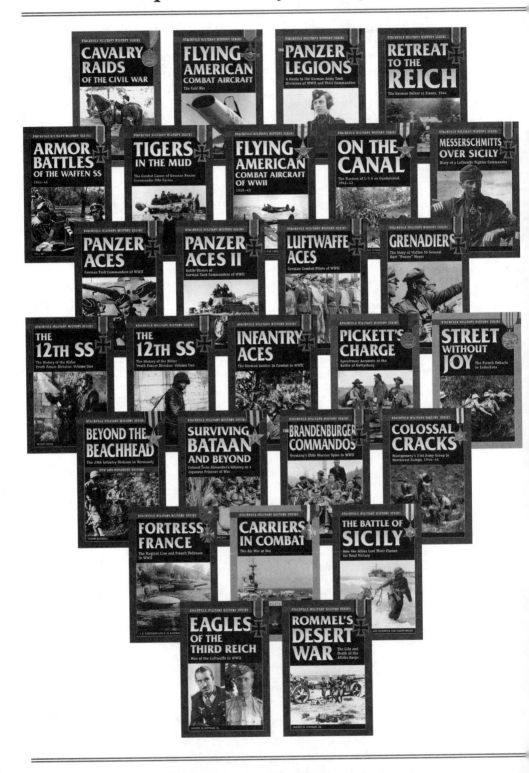

Real battles. Real soldiers. Real stories.

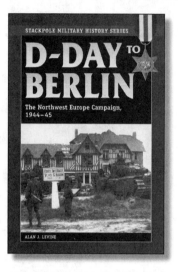

Stackpole Military History Series

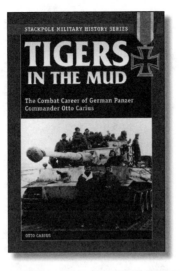

TIGERS IN THE MUD
THE COMBAT CAREER OF GERMAN PANZER
COMMANDER OTTO CARIUS

Otto Carius,
translated by Robert J. Edwards

World War II began with a metallic roar as the
German Blitzkrieg raced across Europe, spearheaded
by the most dreadful weapon of the twentieth century:
the Panzer. Tank commander Otto Carius thrusts the
reader into the thick of battle, replete with the
blood, smoke, mud, and gunpowder so common
to the elite German fighting units.

$19.95 • Paperback • 6 x 9 • 368 pages
51 photos • 48 illustrations • 3 maps

WWW.STACKPOLEBOOKS.COM
1-800-732-3669

Stackpole Military History Series

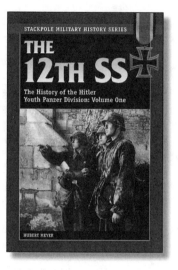

THE 12TH SS
THE HISTORY OF THE HITLER
YOUTH PANZER DIVISION: VOLUME ONE
Hubert Meyer

Recruited from the ranks of the Hitler Youth,
the elite 12th SS Panzer Division consisted largely of
teenage boys who were fanatically devoted to the
German cause. In the aftermath of D-Day in June 1944,
the division received its baptism of fire in Normandy,
launching a fierce counterattack that turned into
a bloody, month-long series of battles for the
French city of Caen.

*$19.95 • Paperback • 6 x 9 • 592 pages • 113 photos,
5 illustrations, 13 maps*

WWW.STACKPOLEBOOKS.COM
1-800-732-3669

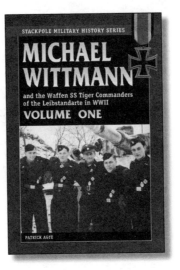

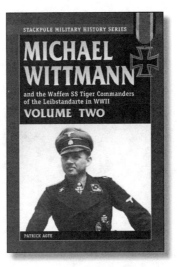

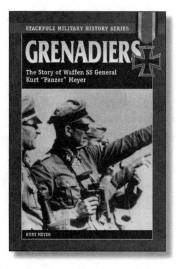

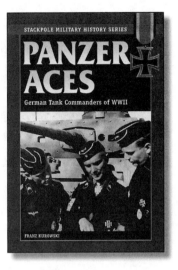